HC 79 . E5

United Nat:
Programme.

The state
environmer

UNEP/GC.14/6

UNEP 1987

Printed by United Nations Environment Programme
P.O. Box 30552, Nairobi, Kenya

ISBN 92 807 1134 2

CONTENTS

PREFACE

One of the main functions assigned to the Governing Council of the United Nations Environment Programme by the General Assembly in resolution 2997 (XXVII) of 15 December 1972 is:

> "To keep under review the world environmental situation in order to ensure that emerging environmental problems of wide international significance receive appropriate and adequate consideration by Governments."

Accordingly, the United Nations Environment Programme issues each year a report on the state of the environment. The first reports published in 1974, 1975 and 1976 discussed a broad sprectrum of environmental issues, such as climatic change, the condition of the biosphere, the effects of toxic substances, food, energy and raw materials, stress and social tension and pollution. At its fourth session, the Governing Council decided that the annual state-of-the-environment report should be selective in its treatment of subjects and that an analytical, comprehensive report on developments regarding each of the issues should be prepared every fifth year (decision 47 (IV), sect. IV, para. 10). Accordingly, subsequent annual state-of-the-environment reports for the years up to 1981 each dealt with a number of selected topics. The criteria for the selection of these topics were set out in the state-of-the-environment report for 1977. In 1982, the United Nations Environment Programme issued, on the occasion of the tenth anniversary of the 1972 Stockholm Conference, the first state-of-the-world-environment report, which covered the period 1972-1982 and dealt with the different changes that occurred in the environment in the decade that followed the Conference. In 1983, 1984 and 1985, the state-of-the-environment reports discussed, again, some selected topics.

At its thirteenth session, the Governing Council of UNEP decided that "future state-of-the-environment reports should, in general, alternate in successive years between a report on economic and social aspects of the environment and a report on environmental data and assessment" (decision 13/9 D, para. 2). The Governing Council further decided in its decision 13/9 D that the 1987 state-of-the-environment report should attempt to present a comprehensive survey utilizing, *inter alia,* the data and results of assessments available through the Global Environmental Monitoring System.

The present report has been prepared in compliance with that decision. Since it is the second "state-of-the-world-environment" report published by UNEP, it has been found appropriate that it should focus on the changes that have taken place in the environment in the period 1981-1986, thereby covering the five years after the first world report. In this respect, I must emphasize that the main focus in the present report has been on the changes (positive and/or negative) that occurred in the different components of the environment with particular attention to the interacting processes between these components.

In the preparation of this report we have relied on relevant information included in reports published by GEMS and other units of UNEP, other United Nations bodies, regional intergovernmental and non-governmental organizations, and some scientific institutions, in addition to scientific publications. Likewise, while we have made an effort to include as much relevant information as possible from countries outside Europe and North America, our ability to do so has been limited by the data available to us and the marked lack of the time-series data required to establish environmental trends. A major publication of UNEP which has to be read in conjunction with this report is our environmental data report, prepared in co-operation with WRI, MARC, IIED and the United Kingdom Department of the Environment.

ii

The present report shows that, over the past five years, there has been a marked improvement in the quality of the data base in certain fields and in our understanding of some environmental phenomena like the possible depletion of the ozone layer or the possible climatic changes. At the same time, however, there are still startling gaps and a special lack of reliable quantitative information about the environment in the developing countries. Fifteen years after the Stockholm Conference, it is clear that we still have an imperfect knowledge of the state of the major components of our environment and of the interacting mechanisms between them. It is my sincere hope that the scientific community will pick up these inadequacies and accelerate the efforts to fill these gaps.

I hope that this report will be found to give a balanced assessment of the world environmental situation as viewed by the United Nations body responsible for the safety and better management of the environment at the global level.

Mostafa Kamal Tolba
Executive Director
United Nations Environment Programme

Nairobi, January 1987

SUMMARY

Over the past five years, there has been a marked improvement in the quality of the data base in certain fields and in our understanding of some environmental phenomena like the possible depletion of the ozone layer or the possible climatic changes due to increases in carbon dioxide and other greenhouse gases. At the same time, however, there are still startling gaps and a particular lack of reliable quantitative information about the environment in the developing countries.

Environmental indicators reveal mixed signals: improvement, stabilization, and deterioration. Thus, air quality monitoring has revealed that there was a general decline in or at least stabilization of carbon monoxide, nitrogen oxides, sulphur dioxide and suspended particulate matter emissions in most urban areas of the developed countries as a result of environmental control measures introduced in the 1970s. Yet, cities like Milan, London, Rome, Brussels, Glasgow and Madrid still have ambient sulphur dioxide in the air above the upper exposure limit established by WHO, and cities like Houston, Sydney, Toronto, Vancouver, Osaka and New York have ambient suspended particulate matter above the upper WHO limit. In general, cities in the developing countries are more polluted with sulphur dioxide and suspended particulate matter than most of the cities in the developed countries.

Recent climate models indicate that the increase in global mean equilibrium surface temperature due to increases of carbon dioxide and other greenhouse gases (especially methane, nitrous oxide and the chlorofluorocarbons, CFC-11 and CFC-12) equivalent to a doubling of the atmospheric carbon dioxide concentration is likely to be in the range of 1.5°C to 4.5°C. Values beyond this range exist but are now usually discarded as non-feasible. A global warming in this range would lead to a sea-level rise of 20-140 cm; a sea-level rise in the upper portion of this range would have major direct effects on coastal areas and estuaries.

A review of the chemical composition of precipitation has revealed no change in the acidity of precipitation in Europe since the 1970s. From 1976 to 1979 there was an increase in acidity of precipitation in the USA but since 1980 there has been no significant change. Acidic precipitation has also been reported in countries in Asia and Africa. Acidic deposition has been implicated as one of the reasons behind the extensive dieback of the forests in Europe. At the end of 1985, there were about 7 million ha of forests in 15 European countries affected to varying degrees. In 1985, a protocol to the 1979 Convention on Long-range Transboundary Air Pollution on the reduction of sulphur emissions or their transboundary fluxes by at least 30 per cent was signed in Helsinki.

Concern regarding the possibility of a reduction in stratospheric ozone due to chlorofluorocarbons (CFCs) remains, although current estimates of such a reduction are lower than those reported a few years ago. It is now believed that if production of CFCs were to continue at the current rate, the steady-state reduction in total global ozone could be about or less than 3 per cent over the next 70 years. The appearance of a hole in the ozone layer over Antartica in spring can be taken as a manifestation of the negative impact on ozone. It has been predicted that a 1 per cent reduction in global stratospheric ozone would lead to an increase of approximately 2 per cent in ultraviolet radiation (UV-B) reaching the Earth's surface; the latter is known to be harmful to biota and human health.

The adoption of the Vienna Convention for the Protection of the Ozone Layer in 1985 is a step towards co-ordinating international efforts to address the threats of the possible reduction of the ozone layer. Efforts are under way, within the framework of that Convention, to conclude a protocol dealing with chlorofluorocarbons.

In general, the overall quality of the water in rivers and streams of the developed countries has improved since the 1970s as a result of legislation particularly the introduction of secondary and tertiary treatment of municipal waste water and the reduction in the discharge of untreated or partially treated waste water into different surface-water bodies. Similarly, there has been a drop in the heavy metal content in most rivers since the 1970s. However, the concentration of nitrates has increased in almost all surface-water bodies. The scattered data indicate that water pollution is a growing problem in many developing countries.

The state of water supply and sanitation continues to be a matter of deep concern. In rural areas of developing countries, 61 per cent of the population did not have reasonable access to safe water supplies in 1983, and 86 per cent did not have sanitation facilities. The respective figures for urban dwellers were 26 per cent and 47 per cent. This continuing grave situation of water supply and sanitation is the main reason for the prevalence of communicable diseases in many developing countries and is also behind the spread of schistosomiasis and malaria, which is resurgent in many areas.

Concern over marine pollution, especially in regional seas has continued. Action plans to prevent the further deterioration of the state of the regional seas and to improve it had been adopted in nine regions by the end of 1986, with the assistance of UNEP. Regional conventions have been signed in eight of the regions (Mediterranean, Kuwait Action Plan, Wider Caribbean, West and Central African, Eastern African, South-east Pacific, Red Sea and the Gulf of Aden, and South Pacific regions). The dumping of low-level radioactive waste in the Atlantic Ocean has been halted since 1983 and has also been prohibited in the South Pacific Ocean under Convention signed in November 1986.

The world's potentially cultivable land has been estimated at about 3200 million ha, half of which is already under cultivation. At present, 5-7 million ha of cultivated land are being lost every year through soil degradation. The World Soils Policy launched by UNEP in 1982 is far from being implemented due to lack of financial resources. A recent assessment by UNEP in 1984 has indicated that about 4,500 million ha are affected by desertification to varying degrees. Currently, each year some 21 million ha are reduced to a state of near or complete uselessness. In Africa, widespread famine, malnutrition and deaths arising from drought and desertification affecting some 21 countries constituted a major crisis that persisted over the past few years. At the peak of the crisis, in 1984 and 1985, an estimated 30-35 million people were seriously affected, of whom about 10 million were displaced.

The total forest area in the world is about 4,700 million ha (about 32 per cent of the total land area in the world). On a global basis, the world's forests are disappearing at the rate of 15 million ha each year, with most of the losses occurring in humid parts of Africa, Asia and Latin America. The average annual rate of deforestation in tropical countries has been estimated at 11 million ha. This deforestation has led to the loss of valuable genetic resources and has created shortages in fuelwood supplies in many areas in developing countries. Although afforestation projects have been undertaken in some countries, the annual rate of afforestation is lagging far behind the rate of deforestation.

The destruction of natural environments is reducing the number of species and the amount of genetic variation within individual species; biological diversity is declining. Of the approximately 265,000 plant species in the world, more than 60,000 are currently in danger of extinction. The protection of wildlife and genetic resources continues to be of major concern to the world. Several conventions now protect wildlife species; the Convention on international Trade in Endangered Species of Wild Fauna and Flora (CITES), administered by UNEP, came into force in 1975. At present, over 90 countries have become parties to the convention. As of 1985 more than 700 species have been on the trade prohibition list of CITES. The nationally designated sites as protected areas increased in number from 2,626 in 1980 to 2,955 in 1985. As of 1985, 243 biosphere reserves had been established in 65 countries and the total number of sites of wetlands considered protected areas within international programmes reached 325.

Although population growth rates have steadily declined, both globally and in the developing countries as a group, regional differences exist. In most of the developing countries there have been marked declines in population growth rates, but in Africa, there has been a marked increase and in South-East Asia and South Asia the population growth rate has remained stable or has declined slightly. Throughout the world, the pace of improvement in infant and child mortality has been slowing down; a pattern that was already evident in the 1970s. Yet, the introduction of oral rehydration therapy (ORT) to treat dehydration in infants has been an important breakthrough, saving the lives of millions of infants in many countries.

Agricultural output and food production have increased only slightly since 1980. World-wide, the average annual rate of growth in food production for the period 1980-1985 was 2.6 per cent. World food production slowed down in 1985 due to a sharp deceleration in growth rate in developed countries. Famine and malnutrition remain widespread, the number of undernourished people is between 340 million and 730 million. Although the introduction of high-yield varieties of grain and modern agricultural management has increased productivity in certain areas, this "green revolution" approach requires HYVs of seeds and high inputs of water, fertilizers and pesticides. These may not be available to all areas, and especially to small farmers. In addition the extensive use of fertilizers and pesticides has created a number of undesirable environmental problems. Further more, the extensive use of HYVs of seeds is expected to lead to a marked decrease in genetic diversity. Efforts are now under way to apply genetic engineering technologies to specific agricultural problems. Yet our knowledge of the environmental impacts of such technologies is still inadequate. Although more than 20,000 edible plants are known, about 20 dominate the world's food supply. Therefore, we need revitalized world-wide investigation of little-known plant species to expand our agricultural resource base and ease our dangerous dependence on a handful of crops.

The industrial sector continues to play a major role in the economic development of many countries. Over the period 1979 to 1985 there have been some important changes in this sector. New high technology industries (robotics, automation, micro-electronics, etc) have become widespread in the developed countries. Such technologies in addition to "cleaner" technologies (like recycling) have created new types of pollution problems. Therefore, there has been a shift from traditional pollutants to more complex toxic pollutants such as heavy metals, toxic air and water pollutants and hazardous wastes. The impacts on human health and the environment from industrial accidents continue to be of concern. The accidents at Bhopal in 1984, the nuclear accident in Chernobyl in 1986 and the explosion at the Sandoz Company in Switzerland in 1986 are examples of serious accidents that can occur and that cause genuine concern for the safety of man and the environment. UNEP is in the process of consultation with Governments, relevant members of the United Nations system and industry to conclude international agreements on notification of industrial accidents and on mutual assistance in case of such accidents.

One clearly positive element that continued to grow over the past years is the public's awareness of the environment. While remaining concerned about pollution, people became more alert to the scarcity of some natural resources, the necessity for conservation and the relationship between environment and development. At present, nearly all countries have environmental machineries of some kind. An increasing number of environmental laws have been formulated and/or updated to control pollution and conserve natural resources. There has been a marked growth in environmental research and development in many countries. In general, the public wants, and in so many cases expressed an interest in participating in securing a better environment.

While the state of the world environment is not directly dependent on short-term economic fluctuations, it cannot be considered to be isolated from them. Owing to the world economic situation, there has evidently been less readiness and capacity on the part of the developed countries to deal with the problems of environmental improvement in the developing countries, or indeed in the developed countries themselves. The world community is confronted by a closed *cycle: economic problems cause environmental despoliation which, in turn, makes economic and structural reform more difficult to achieve. Breaking the cycle requires a new earnestness from nations in their approach to environmental co-operation. Two major causes of environmental destruction should be tackled now. First, the arms race, with its insatiable demands on global financial, material and intellectual resources, must be slowed. The second requirement is to alleviate the appalling debt burden of many developing countries. The expectations for multinational co-operation raised at different forums over the past decade have so far not been realized. In the field of environment, however, the preparedness of Governments to translate good intentions into action has been more positive. The various international agreements concluded over the past few years are illustrations of international support for environmental protection. However, there is still an urgent need for the world community to translate these good intentions into practical action. This is particularly true for the world plans of action such as those relating to desertification control, soils, conservation strategies, the protection of regional marine environments, and others.*

ENVIRONMENTAL QUALITY

Air quality and atmospheric issues

Water quality

The marine environment

Land

Terrestrial biota

ENVIRONMENTAL QUALITY

AIR QUALITY AND ATMOSPHERIC ISSUES

Air quality

1.   Air pollution arises from a multitude of sources. The importance of a particular type of source depends to a certain extent on the location and the climate. No matter where an area is situated it will have in its atmosphere a mixture of pollutants from a variety of sources, such as heating plants (both industrial and domestic), industrial processes, waste incinerators, automobiles, and other transport vehicles. The concentration of air pollutants depends not only on the quantities that are emitted but also on the ability of the atmosphere to absorb or disperse excess amounts.

2.   Air pollution was not perceived as a major problem in most countries until the late 1950s and 1960s. It was then usually still seen as a local problem in urban and industrialized areas. Only in recent years has air pollution evolved as a problem of regional and international importance.

3.   In 1980, global emissions of common air pollutants into the atmosphere as a result of human activities consisted of about 110 million tons of sulphur oxides, 59 million tons of particulate matter, 69 million tons of nitrogen oxides, 194 million tons of carbon monoxide and 53 million tons of hydrocarbons (1). The amounts of pollutants emitted vary from one area to another depending on the density and type of human activity and on the measures adopted to reduce such emissions. As can be seen from figure 1, the countries of the Organisation for Economic Co-operation and development (OECD) account for about half of the total annual global emissions of pollutants.

4.   Most air pollutants enter the body by inhalation, thus making the respiratory system the main part of the body directly affected. The exposure to more than one pollutant at the same time (which is normally the case) can further aggravate health effects; for example, the effects increase synergistically on exposure to both sulphur oxides and particulate matter at the same time. Air pollution has also adverse effects on agriculture, forest growth, water resources and different buildings and structures. Estimates of total annual damage resulting from air pollution reached 1 per cent of the gross domestic product (GDP) in France and 2 per cent of GDP in the Netherlands, for example (1). Although it is difficult to determine the exact impacts of different air pollutants on human health and the environment, ambient guidelines have been established as indicative values for the protection of human health and the environment. The United Nations Environment Programme (UNEP) and the World Health Organization (WHO) have jointly sponsored the publication of environmental health criteria for the common air pollutants (2).

5.   Concern about the different impacts of air pollution has triggered a number of national and international actions in recent years. Programmes have been established, especially in developed countries, to routinely monitor and assess air quality conditions, to observe trends, and to assess the relationship between air pollution and human health. In 1973, WHO established a global programme of air quality monitoring to assist countries in operational air pollution monitoring, to improve the practical use of data in relation to the protection of human health, and to promote the exchange of information. The air

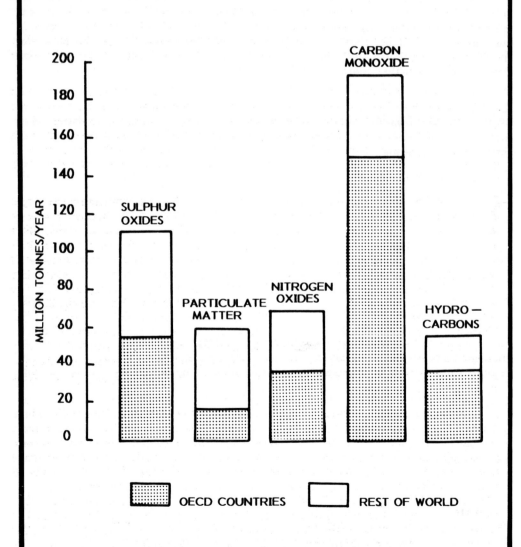

Figure 1.
Total world emissions of common air pollutants from human activities in 1980

Source: Data contained in OECD, The State of the Environment 1985. (Paris, 1985)

monitoring project became a part of the Global Environmental Monitoring System (GEMS) in 1976. At present, some 50 countries are participating in the GEMS air monitoring project in which data are obtained at approximately 175 sites in 75 cities (3), 25 of which are located in developing countries. Measurements at the GEMS project sites have so far been limited to sulphur dioxide (SO_2) and suspended particulate matter as indicators of industrial pollution in urban areas. The data obtained from national air monitoring systems and from the GEMS project indicate certain general trends in urban air quality.

6.   Several countries have had marked success in reducing industrial emissions by installing air pollution control equipment at enterprises. In Bulgaria, for example, emissions of suspended particulate matter were reduced by 1.6 million tons a year in the period 1976 to 1980. In the same period, toxic substances in gaseous emissions were cut by 70 per cent and had been reduced by 81 per cent by 1985 (4). Comparable reductions in air pollutants have been recorded in the German Democratic Republic, Hungary, and the USSR. In some countries, seasonal changes occur in the concentrations of air pollutants: in Hungary, for example, the concentrations of sulphur oxides, nitrogen oxides, and suspended particulate matter in most urban areas are higher in winter than in summer owing to the extensive use of fossil fuels, especially coal, for heating in winter (5).

7.   Trend analyses of *carbon monoxide* (CO) emissions in OECD countries for the period 1970 to 1979 show that the total emissions declined significantly in North America and Japan and that the picture in the European members is mixed. In the period from 1979 to 1984, CO emissions and concentrations in urban areas in the OECD countries declined or at least stabilized, as a result of a levelling off or a slower rate of increase in the total number of vehicle-kilometres travelled by motor vehicles and the effects of the environmental controls introduced in the 1970s (1).

8.   In the period from 1970 to 1979, *nitrogen oxides* (NO_x) emissions from transport sources tended to increase in most OECD countries, while emissions from stationary sources remained relatively stable. From 1979 to 1984 there was a decline in or at least a stabilization of NO_x emissions in most OECD countries, which has been attributed to stagnation in GDP or reduced rates of economic growth, greater efficiencies of national economies with regard to fossil fuel requirements as a result of energy savings and a greater reliance on alternative sources of energy, and the environmental control measures introduced in the 1970s. The level of NO_x emissions is likely to remain stable up to 1990 but may be more significantly reduced in many OECD countries by 1993, following the resolution adopted at the Multilateral Conference on the Causes and Prevention of Damages to Forests and Waters by Air Pollution in Europe, held at Munich in June 1984. Negotiations are also under way among member States of the Economic Commission for Europe (ECE) on a protocol on the control of NO_x emissions within the framework of the 1979 Convention on Long-range Transboundary Air Pollution (1).

9.   Over the period from 1970 to 1979, *sulphur dioxide* (SO_2) emissions fell significantly in most OECD countries and the downward trend continued in most of these countries from 1979 to 1984, for largely the same reasons as NO_x emissions fell over the same period (see paragraph 8 above). Ambient concentration levels of sulphur dioxide have also decreased in most cities of the OECD countries, with the exception of Rome, Italy, where ambient sulphur dioxide concentration increased from 74 micrograms per cubic metre (ug/m^3) in 1980 to about 90 ug/m^3 in 1982 (1), which is well above the upper exposure limit established by WHO. (Figure 2 illustrates the trends in sulphur dioxide concentrations in a number of urban cities in OECD countries.) As a result of the protocol on the control of sulphur emissions signed in Helsinki in 1985, it is likely that by 1993 many of the OECD countries will have reduced their emissions by at least 30 per cent of the 1980 levels.

4

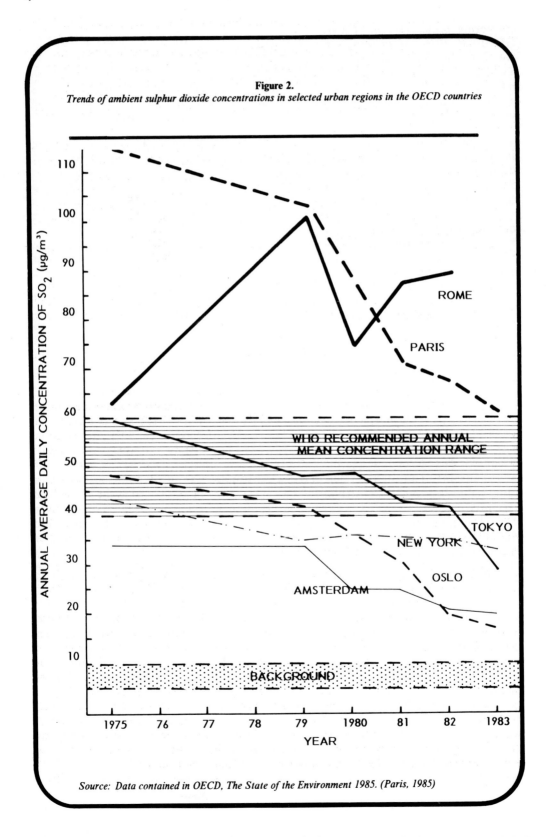

Figure 2.
Trends of ambient sulphur dioxide concentrations in selected urban regions in the OECD countries

ANNUAL AVERAGE DAILY CONCENTRATION OF SO_2 ($\mu g/m^3$)

ROME

PARIS

WHO RECOMMENDED ANNUAL
MEAN CONCENTRATION RANGE

TOKYO

NEW YORK

OSLO

AMSTERDAM

BACKGROUND

1975   76   77   78   79   1980   81   82   1983

YEAR

Source: Data contained in OECD, The State of the Environment 1985. (Paris, 1985)

10.   On a global basis, trend analyses carried out for data obtained from 63 of the GEMS air monitoring sites (all with data for five years or more) showed downward trends in sulphur dioxide concentrations at 54 per cent of the sites, upward trends in 16 per cent, and stationary levels at 30 per cent over the period 1973-1980. The mean values of sulphur dioxide concentrations for the period 1975-1980 indicate that 49 per cent of the sites are below the lower exposure limit established by WHO (40 ug/m^3), 25 per cent are within the WHO guideline values (40-60 ug/m^3), and 26 per cent of the sites are above the upper exposure limit (60 ug/m^3).

11.   Emissions of suspended particulate matter showed a significant decline in most OECD countries from 1970 to 1984. Trend analyses of data obtained from 62 GEMS air monitoring sites show that over the period 1973-1980, the average annual concentration of suspended particulate matter decreased in 43 per cent of the sites, increased in 10 per cent, and remained stationary in 47 per cent. The average concentrations taken in the measurement period 1975-1980 from all sites in the GEMS project show that 24 per cent of the sites are below the lower exposure limit established by WHO (40 ug/m^3), 34 per cent are within the guideline values (40-60 ug/m^3), and 42 per cent are above the upper limit (60 ug/m^3).

12.   The data obtained from the GEMS air monitoring project show that most cities in the developing countries are more polluted with sulphur dioxide and suspended particulate matter than most cities in the developed countries. However, the available data do not allow for trend analyses since they generally cover only a short period of time (less than 5 years).

Acidic deposition

13.   First raised as an international problem by the Scandinavian countries at the United Nations Conference on the Human Environment, acidic deposition has developed into a major international environmental issue. A great deal of research has been carried out over the last decade and ample information has been made available through the Co-operative Programme for Monitoring and Evaluation of Long-range Transmission of Air Pollutants in Europe (EMEP), under the 1979 Convention on Long-range Transboundary Air Pollution and through activities conducted in accordance with the Memorandum of Intent between the Government of Canada and the Government of the United States of America concerning Transboundary Air Pollution. Furthermore, a special conference on acidification of the environment was held in Stockholm in 1982, followed by a second major international conference in Munich in 1984. Both conferences reviewed and assessed a large amount of up-to-date scientific information on acidic deposition.

14.   In the last 10 years, the United States, Canada and several European countries have established monitoring stations to determine the composition of acidic deposition. On a global scale, the WMO Background Air Pollution Monitoring Network (BAPMoN), which started operation in 1972 and is now supported by GEMS, involved 95 countries at the end of 1986. About 70 of these countries had operational stations, and 55 were regularly reporting data related to precipitation chemistry. One outcome of this extensive monitoring activity has been the improved delineation of areas receiving acidic precipitation, as illustrated in figure 3 (6). A 1982 review of the chemical composition of precipitation as measured by BAPMoN (7) pointed out that the spatial distribution of the acidity of precipitation over Europe and eastern United States did not change significantly between 1972 and 1976. In the period from 1976 to 1979, no change was detected in the acidity of precipitation in Europe, while in the United States an increase was recorded. Since about 1980, average annual patterns for wet deposition in the United States have shown few significant changes, reflecting the fact that emissions have remained relatively constant (8). Recent studies have indicated that acidic precipitation occurs also in Japan, India, China

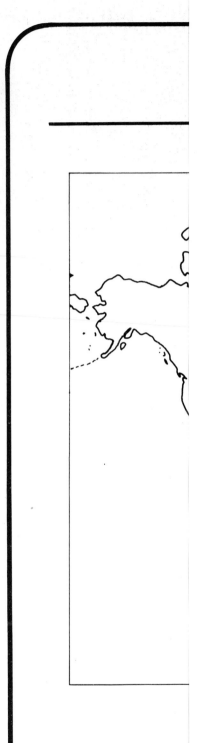

Source: D.M. Whelpdale, "Acid

and some developing countries in Asia and Africa (9, 10, 11). Hungary experiences both wet and dry acidic deposition, especially in winter (5).

15. Knowledge of the effects of acidic deposition on the environment varies from certain to speculative, but there is a considerable body of evidence to show that acidic deposition poses a threat to various economic resources: fisheries, forestry, agriculture and wildlife. Not all the areas subject to acidic deposition, however, are equally susceptible. The higher the capacity for natural buffering in the soil and water, the greater the ability to neutralize acidic compounds. Effects will be greatest in high-sensitivity areas exposed to high deposition.

16. Hundreds of lakes in parts of Scandinavia, the north-east United States, south-east Canada and south-west Scotland have been affected by acidic precipitation. Recent surveys have shown that in the United States damage from acidic deposition has occurred in roughly 50 per cent of 219 high-elevation lakes studied in the Adirondacks (12). In Ontario, Canada, over 300,000 hectares of about 11,400 lakes are considered to be at moderate to high risk, representing a potential loss of 30 per cent or more of the total provincial resource of at least five major fish populations. Most vulnerable were brook trout, lake trout and bass (13).

17. Recently, concern has been expressed over the impact of acidic deposition on drinking water quality. Acidified waters may leach toxic metals from watersheds and water distribution systems, and the presence of these metals in drinking water can result in a number of serious human health impacts (14, 15, 16). Acidification of ground water supplies has been reported from Sweden, North America, the Netherlands and the Federal Republic of Germany (17). In some areas, the pH level of ground water is less than 4.5, and the concentrations of copper, zinc, cadmium and aluminium are often 10 to 100 times larger than in neutral ground water.

18. Acidic deposition can affect forests either directly, by acting on the foliage, or indirectly, by changing the properties of the soil supporting forest growth. Sensitivity varies with species and the buffering capacity of soils. Coniferous forest soils are believed to be especially vulnerable (13). Visible injuries to pine forests in Canada have been observed in connection with growing-season concentrations of around 45 ug of sulphur dioxide per cubic metre of air. Similar effects have been reported from Czechoslovakia (17).

19. In 1984, it was estimated that about 50 per cent of the total forest area of the Federal Republic of Germany (3.7 million ha) was damaged to varying degrees: about 33 per cent was slightly damaged, 16 per cent damaged, and 1.5 per cent severely damaged and dead (18). This "dieback" of the forests (mainly spruce) in the Federal Republic of Germany has been attributed to various causes: acidic deposition, soil acidification, effects of atmospheric sulphur oxides and nitrogen oxides, ozone (and possibly other photo-oxidants), climate, pathogens, and the effect of ammonium and other nitrogen compounds (17, 18, 19, 20). Similar dieback of forests has been reported from other European countries. At the end of 1985, Earthscan estimated that about 7 million hectares of forests in 15 European countries had been affected to varying degrees. The Federal Republic of Germany is the most seriously affected country followed by Switzerland, Austria, the Netherlands, France, Belgium, Denmark and Sweden. In Eastern Europe, Czechoslovakia is the most seriously affected country with between 200,000 and 300,000 hectares of forests severely damaged or destroyed, while in Hungary about 150,000 ha of forests are damaged to varying degrees (5). Extensive forest damage has also been reported from Poland, the German Democratic Republic and Romania.

20. From the standpoint of human health, the data available indicate a minimal risk to healthy individuals associated with inhalation of sulphuric acid aerosols at ambient concentrations. In sensitive groups (e.g., asthmatics, children and adults with a hypersensitive respiratory system) the possibility of diverse pulmonary effects from short-term exposures to 0.1 mg/m^3 of sulphuric acid aerosols cannot be excluded (21). There are, however, two

main ways in which human health may be affected indirectly: acid deposition may reduce the quality of drinking water, and it may cause changes in the human intake of certain trace elements as the trace element content of fish, meat and agricultural crops is increased (21, 22).

21.   The signing of the Convention on Long-range Transboundary Air Pollution in 1979 provided evidence of the determination of different countries to work together and take the measures needed to cut back sulphur and nitrogen oxides emissions to an acceptable level. By March 1985, 30 countries and the European Economic Community had ratified the Convention. The Ministerial Conference on Acidification on the Environment, held in Stockholm in 1982, helped speed up the ratification process and the initiation of a number of activities to control sulphur and nitrogen oxides emissions. One of the most substantive features of the Stockholm Conference was the Nordic proposal for a general 30 per cent reduction of sulphur oxides emissions from 1980 levels over the 10-year period 1983-1993. In 1985, a protocol to the Convention was signed in Helsinki on the reduction of sulphur emissions or their transboundary fluxes by at least 30 per cent.

Greenhouse gases and climate

22.   Carbon dioxide, along with water vapour, ozone and a variety of other trace gases, is a key factor in determining the thermal structure of the atmosphere. These "greenhouse gases" are fairly transparent to incoming solar radiation but relatively opaque to longer-wave thermal radiation from the Earth's surface. Thus, the theory holds that as the concentration of these gases increases in the air, the solar radiation received at ground level will not be markedly reduced, whereas the loss of the thermal radiation from land and water surfaces to space will drop significantly, with the result that there will be a surplus of energy available at ground level, and surface air temperatures will rise.

23.   Current annual emissions of carbon dioxide due to combustion of fossil fuels have been estimated at about 5 billion tons of carbon (23, 24). Terrestrial biota, especially forests and their soils, have been a net source of carbon dioxide for the atmosphere over the past century and are currently releasing between 1 billion to 2 billion tons of carbon annually, of which nearly 80 per cent is due to deforestation, especially in the tropics (25).

24.   Estimates of future carbon dioxide emissions vary widely according to future scenarios of energy consumption and the state of the biosphere. It has been estimated that annual emissions of carbon dioxide due to fossil fuels might range between 7 and 13 billion tons of carbon in the year 2000, and between 10 and 30 billion tons of carbon in 2030 (23). Taking into account past changes in terrestrial ecosystems due to human exploitation of land, the total amounts of carbon in these systems, and the present rates of change, it is plausible to assume that an additional amount of 1-2 billion tons of carbon may be transferred annually to the atmosphere in the period 1980-2100 (25).

25.   The concentration of carbon dioxide in the atmosphere has varied over the ages. Recent analyses of air trapped in glacier ice cores revealed that atmospheric carbon dioxide concentration around the year 1750 was 280 parts per million by volume (ppmv) (26). Precise and continous measurements of atmospheric carbon dioxide have been made since 1958 at Mauna Loa Observatory, Hawaii, and show a clear increase from 315 ppmv in 1958 to 343 ppmv in 1984 (27). If the present rate of increase of carbon dioxide emission (an average of 1-2 per cent per year since 1973) continues over the next four decades with a slackening thereafter, the carbon dioxide concentration towards the end of the next century will be twice the pre-industrial level (or about 600 ppmv) (24).

26.   The most important trace gases that would contribute to the greenhouse effect are nitrous oxide, methane, chlorofluorocarbons (especially CFC-11 and CFC-12), ozone, and water vapour (28, 29). The total annual emissions of nitrous oxide have been estimated at about 30 million tons, 25 per cent of which are anthropogenic (29). Measurements of nitrous oxide concentration in the atmosphere show an increase from 289 parts per billion by volume (ppbv) in 1970 to 303 ppbv in 1984 (27). It has been estimated that the nitrous oxide concentration might reach 375 ppbv in the year 2030 (28).

27.   The total amount of methane emitted annually into the atmosphere has been estimated at about 550 million tons, about half of which comes from anthropogenic activities (29, 30). Most of the methane emitted into the atmosphere (about 90 per cent) is removed through oxidation, the balance remains airborne. The concentration of methane in the atmosphere in 1980 was about 1.65 ppmv in the northern hemisphere and about 1.55 ppmv in the southern hemisphere (29,30). Globally averaged concentrations of methane increased from about 1.52 ppmv in 1977 to about 1.65 ppmv in 1985 (31). The concentration of methane in the atmosphere increased by about 0.5 per cent per year between 1965 and 1975 and by 1-2 per cent per year after 1978 (30), and it has been estimated that the methane concentration in the atmosphere might reach 2.34 ppmv in the year 2030 (28).

28.   Chlorofluorocarbons (CFCs), especially CFC-11 and CFC-12, have been emitted from industrial sources to the atmosphere during the past 50 years. It has been estimated that the annual emission of both CFC-11 and CFC-12 is about 400,000 tons (29). The concentration of CFC-11 in the atmosphere was about 150 parts per trillion by volume (pptv) in 1977 and had reached 230 pptv (27). The CFC-12 concentration rose from 260 pptv in 1977 to 400 pptv in 1985, and it has been estimated (28) that the concentration of CFC-11 and CFC-12 in the atmosphere might reach 1100 pptv and 1800 pptv, respectively in the year 2030.

29.   An evaluation of results from recent climate models indicates that the increase in global mean equilibrium surface temperature due to increases of carbon dioxide and other greenhouse gases equivalent to a doubling of the atmospheric carbon dioxide concentration is likely to be in the range of 1.5°C to 4.5°C. (24). Values beyond this range exist but are now usually discarded as non-feasible. Figure 4 presents one possible scenario of cumulative surface warming by the year 2030.

30.   An analysis of surface temperature records during the past 100 years indicates a global warming from the late nineteenth century to about 1940 and a cooling until the mid-1960s. Since then, the world as a whole appears to have warmed. These analyses suggest that the global mean temperature has increased O.3°C to O.7°C in the past 100 years. This increase in temperature cannot be ascribed in a statistically rigorous manner to the increasing concentration of carbon dioxide and other greenhouse gases in the atmosphere although the magnitude is within the range of predictions (24).

31.   Changes in climate that may result from increases in atmospheric carbon dioxide and other trace gases may affect the environment in a number of ways. Since it is not possible at present to make a detailed and accurate prediction of future climatic changes in the different regions of the world, it is possible only to speculate about the impact of changes in climate (24, 32). It is estimated on the basis of observed changes since the begining of this century, that global warming of 1.5°C to 4.5°C would lead to a sea-level rise of 20-140 centimetres. A rise in the upper portion of this range would have major direct effects on coastal areas and estuaries. A significant melting of the west Antarctic ice sheet leading to a much larger rise in sea level, although possible at some future date, is not expected during the next century. (24).

32.   The stability and distribution of food production could be greatly affected by climate warming. In general, the direct effects of increased carbon dioxide concentrations on crop yield are beneficial (33, 34, 35). However, crops are substantially affected by changes in

12

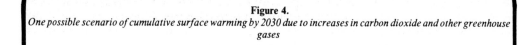

Figure 4.
One possible scenario of cumulative surface warming by 2030 due to increases in carbon dioxide and other greenhouse gases

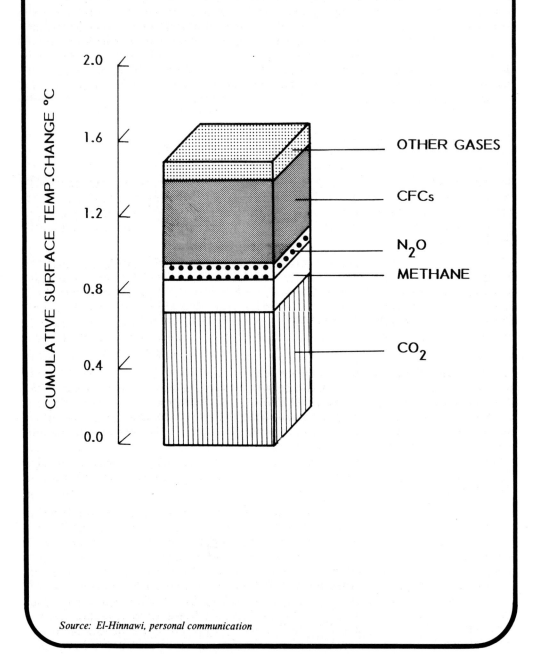

Source: El-Hinnawi, personal communication

climate. Given current technology and crop varieties, a sudden warming of 2°C with no change in precipitation might reduce average yields by 3 to 17 per cent (35). Warmer and longer growing seasons induced by climatic changes could enable many insect pests to pass through an additional one to three generations. The exponential increase of some pest populations under the new favourable environments could increase losses due to insects and make control more difficult.

33.   Models of agricultural production and trade suggest that numerous feedback mechanisms exist in many regions through which agriculture can adjust and adapt to environmental change. Over the long term, food production in such areas appears more sensitive to changes in technology, prices or policy than to those in climate changes, and these factors are largely controllable, whereas climate is not. However, for some regions, particularly marginal lands in the developing world, agriculture may be acutely sensitive to climatic changes, as evidenced by the toll exacted by year-to-year variations in climate. If these regions can adopt measures to reduce further the ill-effects of current, short-term climatic variability, it is likely that they will be better prepared to adapt to any ill effects of future changes that might occur.

Changes in atmospheric ozone

34.   Ozone (O_3)) in the stratosphere is the natural filter that absorbs the sun's ultraviolet radiation (UV) that is harmful to life. Ozone is destroyed in several complex series of chemical reactions (as many as 200 have been identified) involving oxygen, hydrogen, chlorine and nitrogen compounds, with the last three acting as catalysts at very small concentrations.

35.   It has been realized that human activities result in the addition of certain compounds to the atmosphere that upset the balance between the production and destruction processes of ozone, thus leading to changes in the total amounts of ozone above the Earth's surface. The most important of these compounds are chlorofluorocarbons (especially CFC-11 and CFC-12), carbon tetrachloride and methyl chloroform, all of which are chemically inert in the lower atmosphere, but in the stratosphere they are decomposed by ultraviolet radiation to release chlorine, which acts as a catalyst in the ozone destruction process.

36.   At present, the concentration of chlorine in the stratosphere is determined mainly by man-made sources of CFC-11, CFC-12, carbon tetrachloride and methyl chloroform, the atmospheric concentrations of which as of late 1985 were about 230 pptv, 400 pptv, 125 pptv and 130 pptv, respectively (27). The concentration of stratospheric chlorine is expected to rise eventually to about 10 ppbv if the release rates of chlorocarbons remain at the present levels. Although such chlorine emissions are thought to influence ozone primarily in the region above 30 km, it has been argued (36) that important reductions in ozone could take place also below 30 km if the concentration of chlorine were to rise above that of nitrogen oxides (which cause an increase in ozone).

37.   Emissions of bromine could also lead to a significant reduction in stratospheric ozone (36). The production of methylbromide has increased four to fivefold since 1972 and may be expected to rise further if it replaces ethylene dibromide as a fumigant. The use of bromo-fluorocarbons (FC-1301 and FC-1211) as fire extinguishers is growing, and concentrations of these gases in the atmosphere appear to have increased at a rate higher than 10 per cent per year from 1978 to 1983 (36). With the present concentrations of chlorine and nitrogen oxides, an increase in bromine from 0.020 ppbv to 0.10 ppbv is calculated to cause a 4 per cent reduction in the column density of ozone. Effects of chlorine and bromine are nearly additive. For a chlorine concentration of 16 ppbv, the reduction in ozone is predicted to grow from 18 per cent to 23 per cent, as bromine is increased from 0.020 to 0.10 ppbv.

14

38.   Observing the changes in the chemistry of the stratosphere due to the release of trace gases is difficult. The substances of interest are present in only trace amounts, and many of them are difficult to measure. The approach to the problem has been to develop theoretical models of the physical and chemical processes thought to be important in the stratosphere. These models are used to calculate the concentrations of various species as a function of position and time.

39.   Over the past few years, research has led to considerable improvement in our understanding of the effects on stratospheric ozone of releases of chlorofluorocarbons and oxides of nitrogen. Concern regarding the possibility of a reduction in stratospheric ozone due to CFCs remains, although current estimates of such a reduction are lower than those reported a few years ago (27, 31). The latest scientific findings (23, 27, 31) indicate that if production of CFCs were to continue into the future at the current rate, the steady-state reduction in total global ozone could be about or less than 3 per cent over the next 70 years. If the release rate of CFCs should become twice the current level or if stratospheric chlorine reaches 15 ppbv, it has been predicted that there will be a 3 to 12 per cent reduction of the ozone column, assuming that the annual rates of increase in the atmospheric concentrations of carbon dioxide, nitrous oxide and methane continue at their current rates. It should be noted, however, that the calculated effects over longer periods are sensitive to assumed source gas scenarios, and future changes in relative concentrations of these gases may significantly alter current estimates (27). Current models of combinations of pollutants suggest that the reduction in total ozone to date resulting from human activities is less than 1 per cent. Examination of historical data has not yet shown a significant trend in total ozone that can be ascribed to human activities.

40.   Recent measurements have, however, indicated a considerable decrease (about 40 per cent) in the total column of ozone in the lower stratosphere between 15 and 20 km above Antarctica (referred to as the ozone hole). The data indicates that the decrease in ozone occurs in late August and September, remains constant during October, and recovers during the final warming in November. This phenomenon is claimed to have been taking place since 1957 with most of the decrease occurring since the mid-1970s. Measurements taken by NASA have also indicated that there has been a significant decrease of ozone in the latitude belt between 45°S and 70°S. A key question is whether the behaviour in Antarctic ozone is an early warning of future changes in global ozone or whether it will always be confined to the Antarctic region owing to its unique geophysical conditions. Another key question is whether the phenomenon has been induced by human activities or whether it is due to an unexplained natural cycle. More recently, NASA analyses of data received from instruments aboard the Nimbus-7 satellite show that the northern hemisphere is experiencing a decline in atmospheric ozone. The area of greatest decline is centred over Spitzbergen, half-way between Scandinavia and the North Pole. The average annual decrease of ozone has been estimated at 1.5 to 2 per cent.

41.   It has been predicted that 1 per cent reduction in global stratospheric ozone will lead to an increase of approximately 2 per cent in UV-B radiation, which is known to be harmful to biota and human health (31). In addition, substantial reductions in upper stratospheric ozone and associated increases in ozone in the lower stratosphere and upper troposphere might lead to undesirable global perturbations in the Earth's climate. The vertical redistribution of ozone may warm the lower atmosphere and reinforce the "greenhouse" effect associated with an increase in carbon dioxide.

42.   Efforts to address the possible threats of the depletion of the ozone layer led to the adoption of the Vienna Convention for the Protection of the Ozone Layer in 1985. The purpose of the Convention is to promote information exchange, research and systematic observations to protect human health and the environment against adverse effects resulting

or likely to result from human activities which modify or are likely to modify the ozone layer. Further work on the formulation of a protocol on the control of chlorofluorocarbons is under way.

WATER QUALITY

Surface- and ground-water quality

43.   It is commonly stated that some 97 per cent of the Earth's water is in the oceans and that 3 per cent is on land. Of the latter some 77 per cent is stored in ice caps and glaciers, 22 per cent in ground water, and remaining tiny fraction is present in lakes, rivers and streams. A substantial proportion of the ground-water stock lies below 800 m indepth, and is beyond man's present capacity to exploit.

44.   Global water use breaks down into three broad categories: irrigation (73 per cent), industrial uses (21 per cent) and public use (6 per cent). However, water use patterns differ significantly from one country to another. In the developed countries, industries account for 40 per cent or more of all water use, while in the developing countries, the overwhelming bulk of water goes to irrigation. Total annual water use, estimated at 2,600-3,000 km^3 in 1980 (37), reached about 3,500-4,000 km^3 in 1985, an average rate of increase of about 6 per cent a year.

45.   Surface and ground water is subject to pollution from different sources. The basic type of pollution is that caused by the discharge of untreated or inadequately treated waste water into rivers, lakes and reservoirs. With the growth of industry, industrial waste waters discharged into water bodies have created new pollution problems. Toxic chemicals compounds have killed aquatic biota in many water bodies and have rendered waters useless. Another water quality problem is the increasing eutrophication of rivers and lakes caused mainly by the runoff of fertilizers from agricultural lands.

46.   Water quality monitoring has been introduced in several countries—the GEMS water quality monitoring project, initiated in 1976, currently involves about 450 stations in 59 countries—but the data obtained, particularly from developing countries, are in most cases too incomplete to allow trends to be established. Some conclusions may, however, be drawn from the data gathered from a number of monitoring stations in the OECD countries.

47.   The general water quality in the OECD countries (as measured by the amount of dissolved oxygen in a river or lake and the amount of biological oxygen demand (BOD) from the introduced waste) has improved since the 1970s. For example, the BOD level in the Mississipi dropped from 2.4 mg/l in 1970 to 1.1 mg/l in 1983; in the Rhine, it dropped from 6.1 mg/l in 1970 to 2.0 mg/l in 1983 (1). This has been attributed to the effects of clean water legislation introduced, particularly the introduction of secondary (biological) and tertiary (chemical) treatment of waste water, and the reduction in the discharge of untreated or partially treated waste water into different surface water bodies. The 42 rivers monitored in the OECD countries since 1970 have also shown improvement as regards certain other pollutants. For example, the amount of lead in the Rhine dropped from 24 ug/l in 1970 to 8 ug/l in 1983; the amount of chromium dropped from 40 ug/l to 9 ug/l in the same period, and the amount of copper dropped from 24 ug/l to 19 ug/l (1). On the other hand, the concentration of nitrates increased in most rivers. In the mississipi, for example, the nitrates increased from 0.98 mg nitrogen/l in 1975 to 1.58 mg nitrogen/l in 1983; in the Rhine, nitrates increased from 1.82 mg nitrogen/l in 1970 to 3.88 mg nitrogen/l in 1983 (1).

48. In the developing countries, the situation differs markedly from one country to another. The scattered data available indicate that water pollution is a growing problem in many countries. In India, for example, about 70 per cent of the surface water is polluted. China's rivers also seem to be suffering from increasing pollution loads, with 54 of the 78 rivers monitored are reported to be seriously polluted with untreated sewage and industrial wastes. It has also been reported that more than 40 major rivers in Malaysia are so polluted that they are nearly devoid of fish and aquatic mammals, the main pollutants being oil palm and rubber processing residues, sewage, and wastes from other industries (38).

49. Marked progress has been made in water management, especially in the OECD and CMEA countries. Water consumption, particularly in industry has been cut down by recycling and the introduction of more water-efficient processes. For example, about 54 per cent of water used in industry in Bulgaria is now recycled (4), while in the German Democratic Republic, up to 25 per cent of the water used in industry has been saved through better management and recycling (39). Similar achievements have been reported from the Federal Republic of Germany, France and several other countries.

50. Ground water is extensively used in some parts of the world. For example, more than 50 per cent of the drinking water supply and 80 per cent of the rural domestic and livestock water needs of the United States are supplied by ground water (40). According to the United States Geological Survey, ground water use increased in the United States from about 133 million m^3/day in 1950 to about 360 million m^3/day or about one fifth of total freshwater use in 1985.

51. A great deal of concern has been recently expressed over pollution of ground-water resources, and the possibility of over-exploitation of some of these resources. Nitrates in ground water have become a cause of concern in some European countries and in the United States. In Denmark, for example, the overall level of nitrate concentration in ground water has trebled within the last 20-30 years owing to the increased use of fertilizers and manure in agriculture (see figure 5). Water becomes unsuitable for potable use by infants when nitrate concentrations exceed 45 mg/l, and such levels can at times be reached in shallow ground water in agricultural areas.

52. Despite their low solubility, organochlorine pesticides are toxic, and ground water containing even a few parts per billion of these compounds may be unsafe for drinking purposes. By the early 1980s, several incidents of ground-water contamination resulting from the field application of pesticides had been confirmed in parts of the United States such as California, New York, Wisconsin and Florida (41). The most widespread problems involved the insecticides/nematocides aldicarb and DBCP (debromochloropropane). Overall, the emergence of the problem of pesticide residues in ground water adds a new dimension to public health, environmental protection, pesticide innovation and marketing, and agricultural management.

53. Industrial wastes reach ground water from impoundments or lagoons, spills, pipeline breaks and land disposal sites. Recent estimates revealed that in the United States there are 76,000 active industrial landfills, mostly unlined, from which contaminants may leach to ground water (42). Abandoned landfill sites have also been found in some European countries. For example, in Denmark, 3200 sites have been found, 500 of them containing chemical wastes; in the Netherlands there are 4000 abandoned sites, 350 of which require immediate remedial action (1). Furthermore, at gasoline stations and industrial facilities in several countries, millions of underground steel storage tanks for petroleum products are not protected against corrosion. Leaking underground gasoline tanks may be losing millions of litres of gasoline each year, some of which contaminates ground water (43). The United States Environmental Protection Agency found that chemical contamination of ground water has already closed more than 1,100 wells, and that there are about 7,700 sites where ground water has been fouled to varying degrees (43).

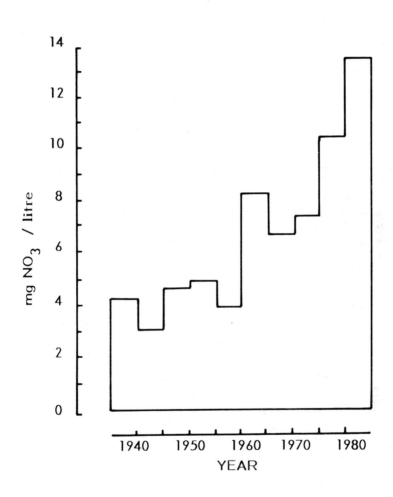

Figure 5.
Distribution of nitrates in ground water in Denmark

Source: J. Forslund, "Ground-water quality today and tomorrow", World Health Statistics
Quarterly, vol. 39 (1986), p. 81.

The state of water supply and sanitation

54. The large number of people with no access to safe, clean water and no sanitation services continues to be a matter of deep concern. Shortages are particularly pronounced in developing countries, especially in rural areas. Although the actual number of people covered by sanitation services has increased slightly, the expansion of services can hardly keep pace with population growth. Thus, a recent WHO survey (44) revealed that in 1983, 61 per cent of the rural population and 26 per cent of the urban population of developing countries did not have reasonable access to safe water supplies. At the same time, 86 per cent of rural people and 47 per cent of urban dwellers were not covered by sanitation services.

55. This grave water supply and sanitation situation is the main reason for the prevalence of communicable diseases in developing countries. Diarrhoel diseases are endemic throughout the developing countries and are the world's major cause of infant mortality. Cholera, typhoid fever, and different intestinal parasites also affect hundreds of millions of people. Studies estimate that the provision of clean water and basic sanitation would reduce the incidence of diarrhoea by 50 per cent, cholera by 90 per cent, sleeping sickness by 80 per cent and Guinea worm infestation by 100 per cent.

56. The lack of clean drinking water and appropriate sanitation is also behind the spread of malaria and schistosomiasis. Nearly half of the world's population—2500 million people—live in areas where malaria continues to be a health risk to some degree. The UNICEF-WHO Joint Committee on Health Policy has estimated that the annual number of clinical cases of malaria in the world is about 95 million, 75 million of which are in sub-Saharan Africa (45). In spite of the early successes in malaria control in the 1960s, the disease is now resurgent in many areas. The parasite *Plasmodium* has developed resistance to drugs and the parasite's vector, the *Anopheles* mosquito has become resistant to DDT and other insecticides. In addition, there has been a marked relaxation in malaria control in some countries. In addition to malaria, schistosomiasis is estimated to affect at least 200 million people and endanger another 600 million in 74 sub-tropical or tropical countries in Asia, Africa, the Caribbean and Latin America. In general, 60 to 70 per cent of all those infected are between 5 and 14 years of age.

57. The International Drinking Water Supply and Sanitation Decade (1981-1990), launched by the United Nations in 1980, is creating a global awareness among policy makers of the importance of safe water supplies and appropriate sanitation in the fight against such diseases. The main objective of the Decade has been to provide all people with clean water supplies and adequate sanitation facilities by 1990. However, a mid-Decade assessment shows that the original goals might not be achieved. It has been estimated that by the end of the Decade only about 79 per cent of people in urban areas and 41 per cent of those living in rural areas will have access to clean water, while only 62 per cent of urban dwellers and 18 per cent of people in rural areas would have been covered by sanitation facilities.

THE MARINE ENVIRONMENT

Marine pollution

58. Most marine pollution reaches the sea from land-based sources, especially from the discharge of municipal waste water and industrial effluents. It also results from the dumping of different wastes in the sea and from incineration of toxic wastes at sea. The main source of marine-based pollution is shipping. Roughly 1.6 million tons of oil annually are discharged

into the sea by shipping. Of the total amount discharged, about 1.1 million tons are non-accidental in origin and are the result of the regular discharge of oil by ships at sea (contaminated ballast water and water used for flushing out tanks). The remainder, about 500,000 tons, is the result of tanker accidents (1). The following table 1 lists the major accidental oil spills that occurred in the period 1980-1984.

Table 1
Accidental oil spills, 1980-1984

Year spilled	Name of ship	Country affected (tons)	Quantity spilled (tons)
1980	Princess Anne Marie	Cuba	6,000
	Irens Serenade	Greece	102,000
	Tanio	France	6,000
	Juan A. Lavalleja	Algeria	40,000
1981	Jose Marti	Sweden	6,000
	Ondina	Federal Republic of Germany	500
	Cavo Cambanos	France	18,000
1983	Castello de Belver	South Africa	255,525
	Sivand	United Kingdom	6,000
	Feoso Ambassador	China	4,000
1984	Assimi	Oman	51,431
	Pericles GC	Qatar	46,631

Source: OECD, *State of the Environment 1985* (Paris, 1985), p. 75.

59. Concern over the dumping of radioactive waste in the sea has increased in the past decade. A number of European countries have been dumping low-level radioactive waste in an area of the Atlantic Ocean at a depth of 4,000 m. Between 1967 and 1982, about 94,000 ton of nuclear waste were dumped (1). The total alpha radioactivity of this waste was about 250 curies in 1967 and had increased to 1428 curies in 1982; the beta-gamma activity was 7,600 curies in 1967 and had risen to about 50,000 curies in 1982. Dumping was halted in 1983, and, in 1985, the parties to the Convention on the Prevention of Marine Pollution by Dumping of Wastes and Other Matter adopted a resolution providing for an indefinite moratorium on low-level waste disposal pending completion of risk-related scientific and other studies. The disposal of radioactive waste at sea is also covered in another recent international agreement—the Convention on the Protection of the Natural Resources and Environment of the South Pacific Region, which was concluded in November 1986 within the framework of the UNEP regional seas programme, and involves twelve South Pacific Island States, France, New Zealand, Australia and the United States. Under the Convention, the parties agree to prohibit the dumping of radioactive wastes or other radioactive matter in the South Pacific Ocean, as well as their disposal into the sea-bed and subsoil of, and their storage in the area.

60.   There are four essential elements needed to evaluate changes in the state of the marine environment. First, standards are required against which the significance of detected changes can be assessed. These may be provided by a baseline study defining the situation at the start of the period under consideration. Secondly, the input of contaminants by man needs to be determined and related to the natural flux of the same materials, including their uptake by organisms. Thirdly, the distribution of these substances in the environment must be monitored in order to detect and follow subsequent changes in contaminant concentrations in ecosystems. Fourthly, ecological studies are needed on the effects of these substances on the marine environment. Given these requirements our knowledge of the state of the marine environment is lacking in several respects. Most monitoring programmes are highly localized and time series data are not available for most areas. As a result, the state of the marine environment and changes to it over time are not easy to determine in general terms with any degree of certainty.

61.   In most cases, sea water quality does not seem to be a valid indicator of the state of the marine environment, and preference tends to be given to measurements based on living organisms (fish, crustaceans, molluscs, algae) or on sediment. However, this is not the case when it is necessary to assess the health risks connected with, for example, bathing, in which case the quality of the sea water itself is assessed to establish the degree of risk for man (pathogenic micro-organisms and micro-organisms indicating faecal pollution) (1).

62.   The discharge of untreated or partially treated domestic waste water into the sea has caused considerable pollution in areas close to major sewage outlets, as is the case in the vicinity of Athens, Barcelona, Venice, Marseilles, New York, San Francisco, Sydney, and other cities (1). Although the danger from this type of pollution is very much limited to areas immediately around the points of discharge (within a few kilometres), it has caused several health problems and economic losses in some coastal areas. The trend now in many countries is to use secondary or more advanced sewage treatment before the effluents are discharged into the sea. For example, in Canada, Japan and the United States, secondary treatment of sewage is carried out in more than 75 per cent of the treatment plants. In Sweden, tertiary treatment is carried out in about 80 per cent of plants (46, 47, 48, 49).

63.   As regards the general level of marine environmental pollution, biological accumulation of potentially toxic substances in sedentary living organisms not only reveals the past history of contamination but also makes it possible to investigate the impact of the pollution control policies pursued on land. A detailed review of the concentration of contaminants in the sea and marine life is contained in the book *The World Environment, 1972-1982,* produced by UNEP in 1982 (37).

64.   To gain a better idea of the state of the marine environment and changes to it, a number of countries have set up systems to monitor the quality of water, of living organisms and of sediments. The United States Mussel Watch Programme uses the physiological characteristics of mussels with regard to the biological accumulation of micro-pollutants as a way of monitoring the changing quality of the marine environment. As a result of that Programme, a fall in PCB concentrations in mussels on the east coast of the United States has been established; high DDT concentrations have been noted on the west coast from San Francisco to San Diego; high concentrations of heavy metals have been found in New York and New Haven; and high concentrations of copper and cadmium have been found in the port of New Haven (1). Similar large-scale national monitoring programmes are carried out by several countries, and most of them have recently become part of regionally co-ordinated monitoring programmes carried out within the framework of specific regional agreements, such as the Oslo and Paris Commissions and the UNEP regional seas action plans and conventions.

65.   The state of enclosed and semi-enclosed regional seas is better understood and seems in general more disturbing than that of the open oceans. Such seas with their highly complex environments are in general characterized by:

(a)   A marine environment which is more sensitive to pollution owing to slow renewal of water and generally limited depth;

(b)   An environment rich in flora and fauna which is often specific to them;

(c)   Strong pressures from what are sometimes highly industrialized coastal countries, that is, human settlements, industry, ports and tourism;

(d)   Intense maritime transport and in some cases the exploitation of mineral and energy resources.

The regional seas, which are usually bounded by several coastal countries, have been the object of extensive international co-operation since the 1970s. With the assistance of the United Nations Environment Programme, action plans to prevent the further deterioration of the state of the regional seas and to improve it had been adopted in nine regions by the end of 1986, and regional conventions had been signed in eight of them (the Mediterranean, Kuwait Action Plan, Wider Caribbean, West and Central African, Eastern African, South-east Pacific, Red Sea and Gulf of Aden, and South Pacific regions).

Marine fisheries

66.   The total world fisheries catch has increased during the past few decades. Between 1950 and 1970, it rose steadily and rapidly at an annual rate of about 7 per cent (total fishery landings were about 62 million tons in 1970). Then, between 1971 and 1972 the total catch dropped, largely due to the dramatic fall in the catches of Peruvian anchovy which was then by far the largest fishery in the world. Since 1972, the catch increased up to 1980, but only at 1-2 per cent annually. From 1980 to 1985, the average annual growth of fish catches reached a high record of 3.2 per cent; the world fish production reached about 84 million tons in 1985 (50). This increase, illustrated in figure 6, was mainly due to substantial rise in catches by South American countries bordering the Pacific Ocean. Two thirds of the fish are destined for human consumption, while the remainder is used either for the feeding of livestock in the form of fish meal or for the manufacture of fertilizers. The FAO estimates that the world catch ought not to exceed 100 million tons per year if the risk of a substantial depletion of fish stocks is to be avoided. However, pressures on stocks in certain areas already amount to overfishing. Overfishing in regions close to the industrial areas of the northern hemisphere, for example, has resulted in a decline in the size and quality of some species of fish and the increasing scarcity of others. Overfishing has led to a sharp drop in catches of cod and herring in particular, the fishing for which in the north-east Atlantic was made subject to quotas in the 1970s and subsequently banned altogether for certain stocks to allow them to recuperate.

67.   By the end of September 1986, 161 countries had signed the 1982 United Nations Convention on the Law of the Sea. Although the United States and several other developed countries have not signed the treaty, the concept of a 200-mile exclusive economic zone is already effectively in operation. Although the new legal regime may appear not to have made a significant impact on fisheries, it may yet play a key role in the management of the ocean's resources. Before the new law, the bulk of the marine fish catch was taken beyong recognized national jurisdiction, which varied from 3 to 12 miles. Management measures could be introduced only through international agreements entered into voluntarily by the countries concerned, and those measures were largely ineffective because they were based on the lowest common denominator. About 99 per cent of the world catch is now taken in water that is already, or potentially, under the jurisdiction of a coastal country. The road to better management, therefore, is now open (38).

22

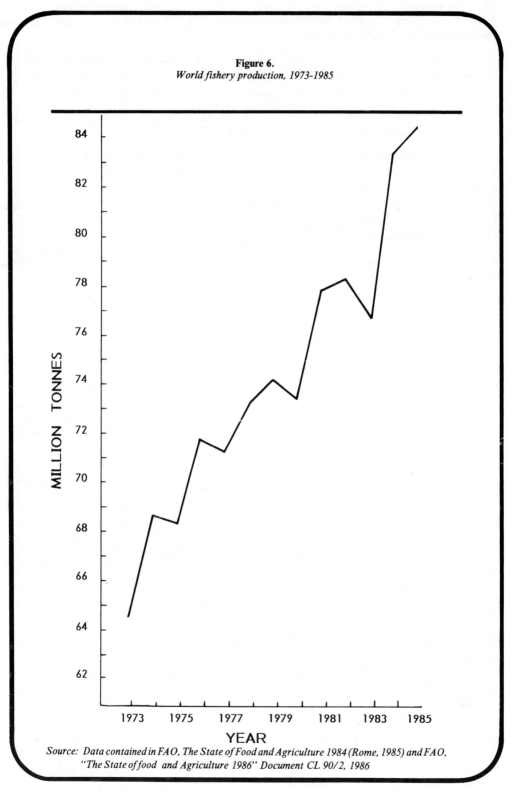

Figure 6.
World fishery production, 1973-1985

MILLION TONNES

YEAR

*Source: Data contained in FAO, The State of Food and Agriculture 1984 (Rome, 1985) and FAO,
"The State of food and Agriculture 1986" Document CL 90/2, 1986*

The status of marine mammals

68.   Marine mammals, including whales, dolphins, seals, and polar bears, have historically been subject to severe hunting. This has caused serious depletion and has even endangered a number of species, although recovery has sometimes occurred where conservation measures have been applied (for example, in the case of gray whales and the Gulf of California and the sourthern right whales of the Valdez Peninsula, Argentina).

69.   Whaling has concentrated successively on single species of whales, and technological development has assured that whales, once located, cannot easily avoid capture. Estimates of the original and current population of the ten species of large whales that have formed the basis of the commercial whaling industry this century in the north Pacific and the southern hemisphere suggest that there is now only about 48 per cent of the total stock of these whales remaining (37). This average figure conceals the fact that while some stocks and species have actually increased during this period as a result of reduced competition among species, whaling has reduced some to five per cent or less of their former numbers. The latest position of the International Whaling Commission (1982), to stop all commercial whaling world-wide from the 1986 coastal and 1985/86 pelagic seasons and onwards and to carry out a comprehensive assessment of the whale stocks by 1990, might indicate a brighter future for the remaining stocks of whales.

LAND

Soil degradation and desertification

70.   Land-use patterns are mainly determined by the interaction between climate, geography, geology and human and economic pressures. In recent decades human modification of land-use patterns has been governed by accelerating requirements for food, fuelwood, and building land. Of the total land area in the world (about 14,477 million hectares, 13,251 million of which is totally ice-free), only 11 per cent (about 1,500 million hectares) is currently under cultivation, while 24 per cent is permanent pasture, 32 per cent comprises forests and woodlands, and 33 per cent is classified as "other" land (51). The world's potentially cultivable land has been estimated at about 3,200 million hectares, about twice the area currently used as cropland. About 70 per cent of potentially cultivable land in the developed countries, and 36 per cent in the developing countries, is currently in use. The situation does, however, vary widely from region to region, for example in South-East Asia, 92 per cent of cultivable land is in use, while the figure for Latin America is only 15 per cent (51).

71.   The productivity of farmland overwhelmingly depends on the capacity of the soil to respond to management. The soil is not an inert mass, but a very delicately balanced assemblage of mineral particles, organic matter, and living organisms in dynamic equilibrium. Soils are formed over very long periods of time, but if their environments are changed (for example, by the removal of vegetation cover), the delicate balance is upset. This can be offset by careful use and management (for example, by the addition of organic matter), but all too often it is not, and a process of deterioration or degradation begins. The degradation of soil, under excessive human pressure or misguided human activity, can occur over a few decades or even years, and is often irreversible.

72.   In recent decades, human management of agro-ecosystems has been steadily intensified, through irrigation and drainage, heavy inputs of energy and chemicals, and improved crop varieties increasingly grown as monocultures. Although bringing some general recent growth in agricultural production, this process has made agro-ecosystems

more and more artificial and often unstable. In addition, overgrazing and overcultivation on steep hillsides and deforestation have increased the loss of vast areas of productive land.

73.   It has been estimated that, against the 1,500 million ha of land currently used for crop production, nearly 2,000 million ha have been lost in historical times. At present, 5-7 million ha of cultivated land (0.3-0.5 per cent) are being lost every year through soil degradation (52). If present trends continue, it seems that all the programmes for adding more land to the food-producing system may not compensate for the areas lost as a result of soil degradation and competing land uses. In other words, cultivated land is being lost at nearly the same rate as new land is brought under cultivation. The FAO study *Agriculture: Toward 2000* calculated that to remedy this situation soil and water conservation measures should be extended to a quarter of all farmland by the end of the century.

74.   Although several countries are adopting certain measures to halt soil degradation and the loss of agricultural land, many of these efforts are not being made within national land use and/or soil protection policies. For example, in Egypt construction on agricultural land has been prohibited by law. In Bulgaria, Hungary and other East European countries, protection of agricultural land is embodied in national development plans and/or nature protection strategies. In the period from 1976 to 1980, more than 740,000 ha of land in Bulgaria were protected from erosion, and over 1.4 million ha were treated to reduce soil pollution (4). In Hungary, soil erosion has caused land degradation in a total area of about 2.3 million ha and efforts are under way to ameliorate the situation (5).

75.   The World Soils Policy launched by UNEP in 1982 is aimed at promoting the environmentally sound management of land and water resources. However, the Plan of Action for the implementation of the Policy is far from becoming operational due to the lack of financial support.

76.   Soil degradation ultimately leads to desertification the global extent of which is reflected in figures 7 and 8. A 1984 assessment by the United Nations Environment Programme indicates that about 4,500 million ha of land are affected by desertification. Estimates indicate that, of this area, 70 per cent is already moderately desertified, and 30 per cent is severely or very severely desertified. The people moderately affected by desertification total about 470 million, while 190 million are severely affected. Currently, each year some 21 million ha are reduced to a state of near or complete uselessness (53). Projections to the year 2000 indicate that a loss on this scale will continue if nations fail to step up remedial action.

77.   Desertification must be seen as a human problem rather than one concerned solely with the deterioration of ecosystems. Desertification is caused almost entirely by human misuse of the environment, particularly in fragile marginal areas with erratic and low annual rainfall. This misuse takes the form of felling trees to provide fuel, overgrazing by domestic animals, and harmful agricultural practices such as planting crops on river banks, which increases soil erosion.

78.   While people are the main agents of desertification, they are also its victim. The most important aspect of desertification lies in its impact on people, on the individual, the family, the community and the nation. The environmental degradation and the biological and physical stress described as desertification in the different dryland livelihood systems have their direct counterparts in physical, emotional, economic and social consequences for man. The effects of desertification on man appear most dramatically in the mass exodus that accompanies a drought crisis. In Africa, widespread famine, malnutrition and deaths arising from drought and desertification affecting some 21 countries constituted a major crisis that persisted over the past few years. At the peak of the crisis, in 1984 and 1985, an estimated 30-35 million people were seriously affected, of whom about 10 million were displaced (54). These figures have been significantly reduced with the recent recovery in crop production in

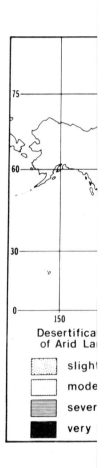

75

60

30

0
150

Desertifica
of Arid La

slight

mode

sever

very

Source: H.E. Dregne, Desertificatⁱ

27

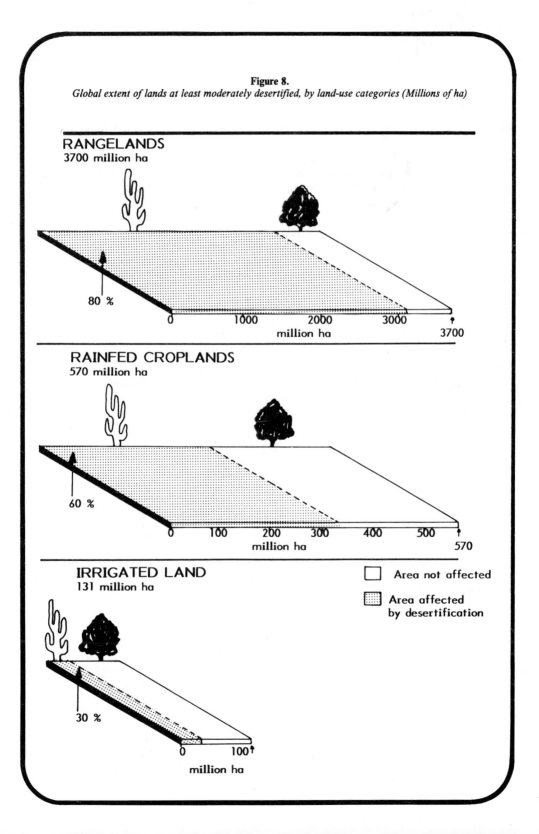

Figure 8.
Global extent of lands at least moderately desertified, by land-use categories (Millions of ha)

several countries. However, chronic malnutrition affecting 150 million Africans, and the general problems of poverty, loss of possessions and resources for meeting minimum needs, which have been building up over the years, remain acute for nearly 20 million severely affected persons in Africa.

Land conversion from agricultural to other uses

79.   The growth of urban areas and inter-city infrastructures has led to a significant conversion of land from agricultural to urban uses in many countries over the past few decades. In the United States, for example, about one million hectares of arable cropland are annually lost to highways, urbanization, and other non-farming uses, although this loss is partially offset by the addition each year of half a million hectares of newly developed cropland (55). Over the period 1970 to 1980, between 1 per cent and 3 per cent of agricultural land in OECD countries was converted to urban use. A large proportion of this land lost to agricultural production was prime farmland of high productivity, on fertile plains or in valleys. The proportion of agricultural land converted to urban uses during the same period reached 2.8 per cent in the United States, 1 per cent in France, 2.5 per cent in Italy and 1.2 per cent in the United Kingdom (1). It has been stated that the economic and environmental cost of continued conversion of the most productive agricultural land in the United States to urban uses could be very high within 20 years. This is in view of the projected increases in demand for the United States agricultural products in the coming years, particularly for exports, and the uncertainty regarding future gains in crop yield per hectare. Similar concerns are expressed in Canada (1).

80.   The absence of land-use policies and land-use planning in many countries, especially in the developing ones, makes it difficult to study the changes in land use with time. One of the objectives of the World Soils Policy has been that land-use plans should be formulated and changes in land use monitored.

TERRESTRIAL BIOTA

Forest resources

81.   Forest cover is of great importance from the ecological point of view. It protects and stabilizes soils and local climates as well as soil hydrology and the efficiency of the nutrient cycle between soil and vegetation. Forests are also the essential habitat of numerous plant and animal species. Virgin forests, especially those in tropical regions, are an irreplaceable repository of the genetic heritage of the world's flora and fauna. From the economic point of view, natural and managed forest resources are utilized in forestry, and timber is also used most importantly for fuel.

82.   Wood has been the primary source of energy for cooking, heating and other basic human needs since prehistoric times, and it remains so in developing countries, in many urban areas as well as in the countryside. Well over two billion people, about half the population of the world, use it for cooking, their most important use of energy. The average person in developing countries uses between 1.3 and 2.5 cubic metres of wood a year (56, 57).

83.   World-wide, about 2.8 billion hectares (or 69 per cent of the forested areas) are covered with closed forests (broad-leaved and coniferous), and 1.3 billion hectares are less densely wooded open forests (38). Natural shrublands and degraded forests in developing countries cover 675 million hectares. When these categories of wooded land are added to open and closed forests, the total represents about 32 per cent of the world's total land area. Figure 9 shows the world distribution of forest areas in 1985.

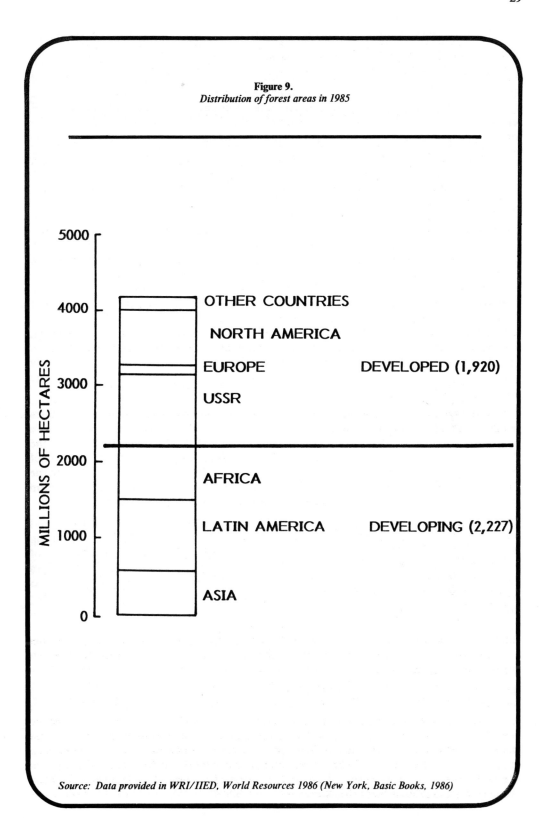

Figure 9.
Distribution of forest areas in 1985

Source: Data provided in WRI/IIED, World Resources 1986 (New York, Basic Books, 1986)

84.   The total stock of wood contained in forests has been estimated at between 340 billion and 360 billion m³. This is the resource base and will eventually be destroyed if more than the annual increment from it, estimated to be 6,610 million m³ (58, 59) is consumed. Official statistics (60) indicate that the total world consumption of roundwood in 1983 was about 3,000 million m³, about 54 per cent of which was used as fuelwood and charcoal (see figure 10). This figure is an underestimate, since many countries keep no accurate records of self-collected or self-produced wood. It would therefore seem the annual increment of the forest resource base can meet the world demand for wood. However, forest resources are very unevenly divided among countries, and although, on a world-wide basis, not all the increment is being removed, much of this unremoved increment is in the inaccessible northern coniferous forests of Alaska, Canada and the USSR. At the same time, there is increasing pressures on, and overexploitation of, forest resources in certain regions, for example, in South-East Asia and Latin America.

85.   Different assessments of the rate of deforestation have been made in the last few years (38, 61). On a global basis, the world's forests are disappearing at the rate of 15 million hectares each year, with most of the losses occurring in humid parts of Africa, Asia and Latin America. The average annual rate of deforestation in tropical countries has been estimated at 11 million hectares (37, 38). African countries account for 62 per cent of the deforestation of the world's open tropical forests and woodlands. With the present rate of deforestation, about 40 per cent of the remaining forest cover in the developing countries will be lost by the year 2000 (1). Yet, in some developing countries, e.g., China, Chile, India, Kenya, significant efforts are being made in re-afforestation. Forests in the temperate zones of the northern hemispheres, although affected by pollution, maintain or even slightly increase their surface because of deliberate efforts to expand forest cover, which include the returning to forests of marginally productive agricultural and pasture land.

86.   Deforestation in the developing countries has created shortages in fuelwood supplies in many areas. By 1980, 96 million people in the countryside of developing countries were acutely short of fuelwood and could not meet their needs (62). The areas affected were the dry land south of the Sahara, East and South-East Africa, various mountainous parts of Africa, the Himalayas, the hills of South Asia, the Andean Plateau, and the arid lands on the Pacific coast of South America. Acute shortages were also felt by a further 150 million people living in cities surrounded by countryside with not enough firewood.

87.   Also in 1980, a further 1,283 million people (about 1,050 million country-dwellers and 231 million urban people) lived in areas where they could get enough wood only by cutting down trees faster than they grow. Seventy million of these people lived in the countryside of North Africa and the Middle East, 143 million in dry parts of the Latin American countryside; 131 million lived in rural Africa south of the Sahara, mainly in savannah areas in the west, centre and south-east of the continent; and no less than 710 million lived in the countryside and small towns of Asia, mainly in the great plains of the Indus and Ganges rivers and in South-East Asia. As long as this situation continues, the trees will steadily disappear, until the people of these areas become acutely short of firewood around the year 2000. By then, of course, populations will have grown and, in all, about three billion people will be facing acute scarcity or will be cutting down trees faster than they grow.

88.   The logical, immediate response to the growing problem of deforestation is to manage existing forests better and to plant more trees. Some countries have recently embarked on afforestation projects: in the Republic of Korea, about 40,000 ha were planted by trees in the period from 1971 to 1976. A 1981 assessment by FAO and UNEP (63) shows that plantations of wood cover about 2.7 million ha in Indonesia, 2.6 million ha in India, 400,000 ha in Bangladesh, 300,000 ha in the Philippines and over 200,000 ha in Thailand. Afforestation efforts are also under way in some European countries: for example, in Hungary 25,000 ha were forested in 1980; in 1984 the area increased to 30,000 ha (5). The United Kingdom has

Figure 10.
Production of industrial wood and fuelwood and charcoal in various regions in the period 1981-1983

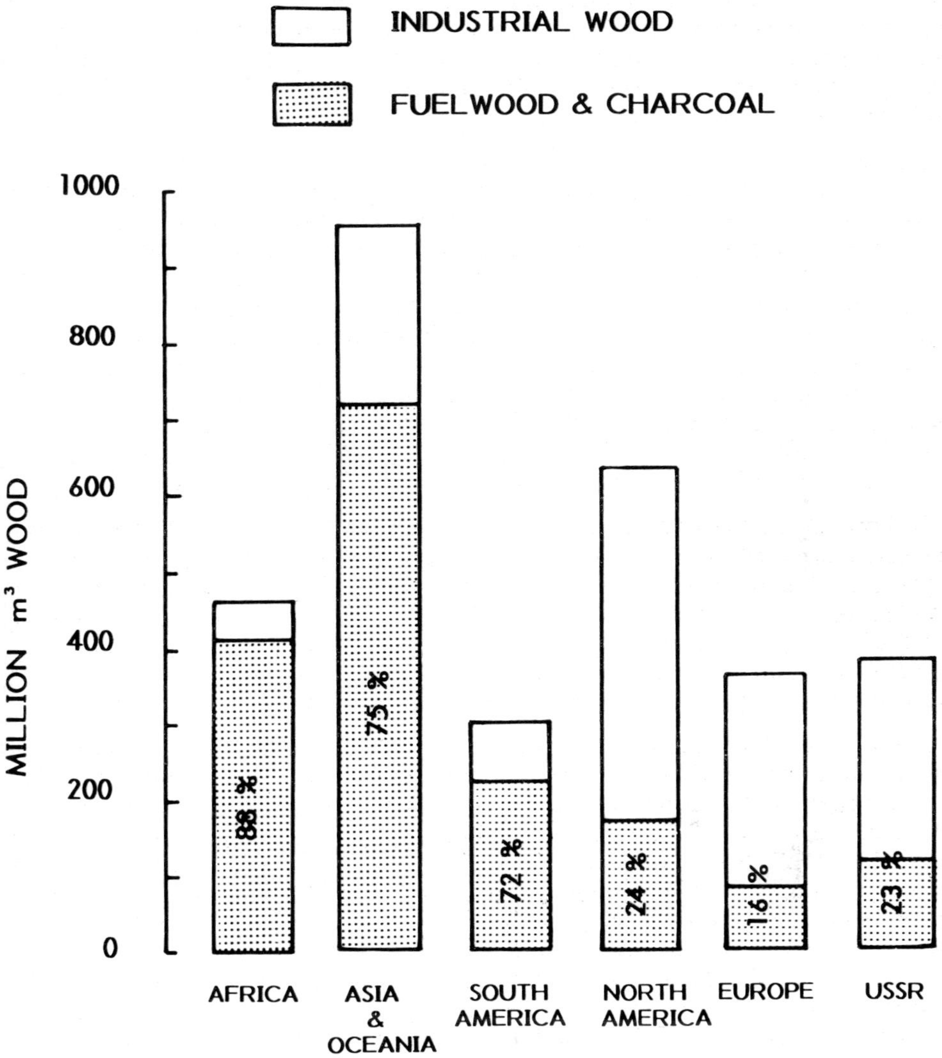

Source: Data provided in FAO, The Yearbook of Forest Products 1981-1983 (Rome, 1985)

announced a target of 30,000 ha per year of new forest planting, to be raised to 35,000 ha in 1987, with a deliberate effort to encourage the establishment of broad-leaved species. Other western European countries have programmes of forest expansion, and the need to reduce agricultural surfaces in those countries is likely to accelerate the process. Despite these and other efforts, no significant changes in the trend of deforestation have been perceived.

Wildlife and protected areas

89.   The world-wide deterioration of natural environments, especially severe in the tropics, is causing the extinction of species at an unprecedented rate. Although 1.7 million species of plants, animals, and micro-organisms have been formally identified and classified, the total number may exceed 30 million, with the great majority living in tropical forests (64). In one area of about 15 hectares of rain forest in Borneo, for example, about 700 species of trees were identified, as many as in all of North America.

90.   It is known that only a tiny fraction of the species with potential economic importance has been utilized. Throughout history, for example, a total of 7,000 kinds of plants have been grown or collected as food. Of these, 20 species supply 90 per cent of the world's food (64). In most parts of the world these few crops are grown in monocultures, particularly sensitive to insect attacks and disease. Yet tens of thousands of species that are edible, and in many cases superior to those already in use, remain unexploited.

91.   Destruction of natural environments is reducing the number of species and the amount of genetic variation within individual species. More than 60,000 of the 265,000 or so plant species are currently in danger of extinction because of the destruction and degradation of the earth's vegetation. The loss is most noticeable in the tropical rain forests. It has been estimated that if a forest area is reduced to 10 per cent of its original size, the number of species that can continue to exist in it will eventually decline to 50 per cent (64).

92.   There are two principal approaches to protecting and managing wildlife: the species approach and the ecosystem approach. The first is concerned with the protection and management of a population or populations of a given species to ensure its abundance and survival. The second is concerned with the management and conservation of a natural community and, therefore, all the species that make up that community. Conservation and management of wildlife resources to date have focused largely on species with known economic value, such as timber and fruit trees, certain marine fish, and game species, especially mammals and birds.

93.   The International Union for Conservation of Nature and Natural Resources (IUCN) lists three major types of threatened species: those *endangered* because of near-term threats to the regenerating populations; those that are *vulnerable* over time because populations are declining in numbers or in geographical distribution; and species that are *rare* because their total population is small or restricted in area. The IUCN Conservation Monitoring Centre maintains data bases on globally threatened species and periodically publishes and updates the *Red Data Books* on major groups of plants and animals. Data from IUCN and OECD show that countries in which more than 30 per cent of the species of mammals are threatened include Austria, Cape Verde, Finland, France, the Federal Republic of Germany, Netherlands, Spain and Turkey. More than 30 per cent of species of birds are threatened in Austria, Netherlands, Spain and Switzerland. As for reptiles and amphibians, more than 30 per cent of the species are threatened in the Federal Republic of Germany, Italy, Netherlands, Spain and the United Kingdom.

94.   Methods of protecting threatened species include legislation, habitat protection, wildlife management, and maintenance of individuals in zoos, botanical gardens, and other artificial habitats. Several international treaties and conventions now protect wildlife

species, but most are bilateral or regional. Among the most far-reaching is the Convention on International Trade in Endangered Species of Wild Fauna and Flora (CITES), administered by the United Nations Environment Programme. CITES came into force in 1975 and now has over 90 parties. The Convention prohibits all trade in species that are believed threatened with extinction and that are affected by trade. The original list of such species consisted of about 370 species, such as the Bengal tiger, the peregrine falcon, the Nile crocodile and many other well-known threatened species. By 1985, more than 700 species had been listed and the range broadened to include plants, such as cacti, orchids and pitcher plants, and a growing number of parrots and tortoises.

95.   The most effective defense against loss of wildlife is to establish and maintain protected areas. Besides national parks, many types of protected areas have evolved in recent years. They range from scientific reserves to multiple-use areas where some exploitation, such as logging or hunting, is permitted. The nationally designated protected areas vary in number from one country to another. In Bulgaria, for example, there were 2,955 protected sites with an area of about 140,000 ha (1.3 per cent of the total area of the country), by the early 1980s (4). In Hungary, the number of protected areas reached 819 by 1985 (5); in the German Democratic Republic there are about 700 protected areas (39); and in Mongolia there are about 30 reserves, of which the Great Gobi Reserve has an area of about 4.5 million ha (65). The number of areas included in the United Nations list of national parks and protected areas increased from 1,478 in 1970 to 2,955 in 1985, covering a total area of about 406 million hectares.

96.   One category of protected area—the biosphere reserve—consists of core areas that receive strict protection, and other zones in which people live and work, usually in farming and forestry. In these reserves, research on both undisturbed and exploited ecosystems is conducted together with environmental education, training, and international scientific exchanges. As of 1985, 243 biosphere reserves had been established in 65 countries, covering a total area of 121 million hectares. Biosphere reserves are an important element in the UNESCO Man and the Biosphere (MAB) Programme. In addition the total number of wetlands sites considered to be protected areas within international programmes reached 325 in 1985.

97.   The World Conservation Strategy published by IUCN, UNEP and WWF in 1980, sets out the three main objectives behind all wildlife policies and practices: to ensure the sustainable utilization of species and ecosystems; to maintain essential ecological processes and life-support systems; and, to preserve genetic diversity. The Strategy emphasizes priorities for national action, including the formulation of national conservation strategies. Currently, some 40 countries have started or completed the formulation of such national strategies. An international conference on the implementation of the World Conservation Strategy convened in Ottawa, Canada in 1986, examined the experience gained at the national level in transforming the principles of the World Conservation Strategy into national plans and recommended that the principal sponsors of the Strategy should revise and update it to take into account these experiences and turn it into a practical tool to achieve sustainable development.

DEVELOPMENT AND ENVIRONMENT

Population growth

Human settlements, transport and tourism

Agriculture and food production

Industrial development

Energy

DEVELOPMENT AND ENVIRONMENT

POPULATION GROWTH

98.   At the beginning of the century there were about 1.6 billion people in the world, by mid-century there were 2.5 billion, and by 1986 this figure had doubled to 5 billion. The world population is expected to reach 6.12 billion by the year 2000. Although the rate of population growth has been steadily falling over the last few years, both globally and in the developing countries as a group (see figure 11), the net absolute annual addition to the number of people is expected to increase from about 78 million at present to about 90 million per year by 2000. Thereafter, with declining net annual additions, the world population may reach 8.2 billion by 2025 (according to the United Nations medium estimate) and reach a stationary level of 10.5 billion by 2110 (see figure 12). The low and high estimates of the stationary population level are respectively 8 billion by the year 2080 and 14.2 billion by the year 2130.

99.   While birth, death and infant mortality rates have fallen consistently, life expectancies have risen in a large number of countries. Some developed countries have already made the demographic transition to population equilibrium, as defined by low birth and death rates a high life expectancies. Many other developed countries and a few developing countries also, show definite movements toward stationary populations.

100.   In many developing countries, both the rate and momentum of population growth have been such as to produce continuous absolute increases in population every year. Even if it were possible to reduce fertility to replacement levels, the momentum of the population would be such that it would continue to grow for many years, because of the young age structure in most developing countries, which means that the number of couples entering their reproductive years will, for a considerable time, remain greater than the number moving out of that age group. Thus, the number of births will continue to be large and to exceed the numbers of deaths.

101.   However, regional differences exist. In East Asia, South-East Asia, Central America and the Caribbean, there have been marked declines in population growth rates. In Africa, by contrast, there has actually been an increase in the population growth rate over the last decade. Of the 58 countries and territories of Africa, 19 show annual growth rates of 3 per cent or more, which imply that populations will double every 23 years, or even more quickly. Population growth rates have continued to decline in tropical Latin America, apart from a few countries; but the declines have been small. In temperate South America, population growth rates have remained nearly constant—at moderate level—over the last two decades. In Asia, growth rates show significant differences from one subregion to another. China, with a quarter of the world's population, has dramatically halved its population growth rate over the last decade. The Repulic of Korea has, likewise, markedly reduced its population growth rate. In South-East Asia and South Asia, the declines have been small. In view of the already large population sizes and decidedly young age structures, the populations of several of these countries are expected to continue to grow substantially.

102.   As for the global distribution, 80 per cent of the increase in the world's population during the last 30 years occurred in the developing countries. What is more, 95 per cent of the entire projected growth to the year 2110—prior to reaching a stationary level of 10.5 billion—is expected to take place in the countries that are currently regarded as

36

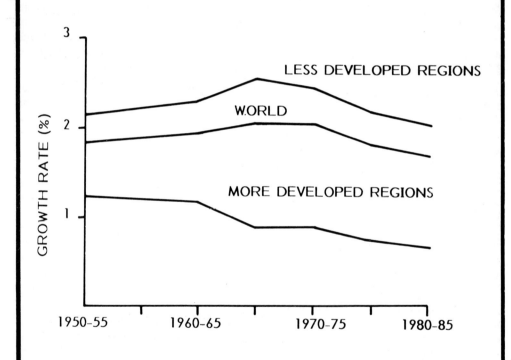

Figure 11.
Average annual population growth rates in more developed and less developed regions, 1950-1985

LESS DEVELOPED REGIONS

W.ORLD

MORE DEVELOPED REGIONS

GROWTH RATE (%)

3

2

1

1950-55   1960-65   1970-75   1980-85

Source: WRI/IIED, World Resources 1986 (New York, Basic Books, 1986).

37

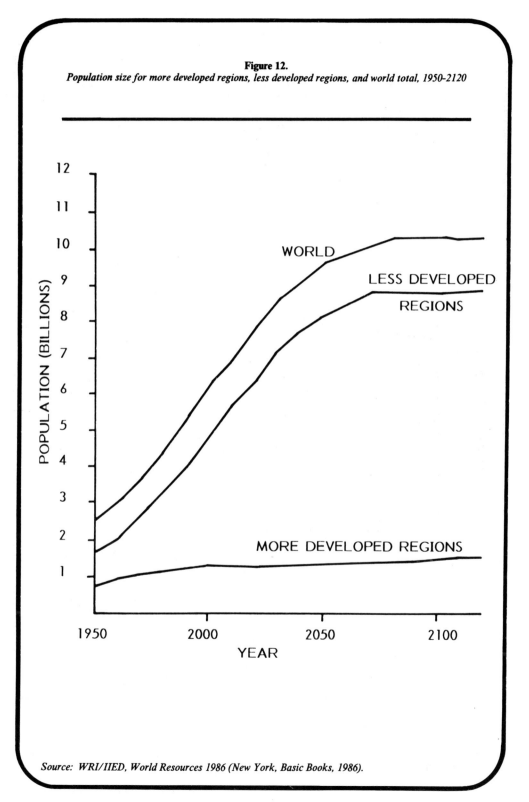

Figure 12.
Population size for more developed regions, less developed regions, and world total, 1950-2120

Source: WRI/IIED, World Resources 1986 (New York, Basic Books, 1986).

developing (66). It is estimated that about 86 per cent of the world's people will be living in today's developing countries when the global population reaches its stationary level. Several developing countries will double, triple or quadruple their populations over the next 50 to 60 years. Africa's relative share of the world population is expected to more than double during the same period (67).

103.   Life expectancy, the number of years a typical individual can expect to live given current levels of mortality, has increased greatly since 1950 and is expected to improve in the future. On a global level, life expectancy increased from 45.8 years in the period 1950-1955 to 58.9 years in 1980-1985, and according to the United Nations projections is expected to reach 70 by the year 2025. Present life expectancy in the more developed countries averaged 73 in 1980-1985, and in the less developed regions it was 56.6; the estimates for 2025 are 77.2 and 68.9, respectively.

104.   As may be seen from figure 13, life expectancy is generally closely related to economic well-being. The countries of South Asia and sub-Saharan Africa tend to have the lowest incomes and the highest mortality rates, while the wealthier countries of Latin America and East Asia have lower mortality. The same relationship holds for infant mortality (see figure 14): poor countries have the highest infant mortality rates. Throughout much of the world, the economic difficulties encountered by many countries and the attendant reduction in expenditure on public health and welfare have meant a slow-down in the pace of improvements in infant and child mortality, a tendency that was already evident in the 1970s. On the other hand, an important breakthrough was made in the first-half of the 1980s, namely the introduction of the simple, effective and inexpensive oral rehydration therapy (ORT) to treat infant dehydration resulting from diarrhoeal disease. In the developing countries, an estimated five million children under 5 years of age—about 10 every minute—died as a consequence of diarrhoeal disease in 1980. The introduction of ORT has saved the lives of millions in many countries. For example, a pilot project carried out in Alexandria, Egypt, showed that the wide introduction of ORT has reduced the death rates of infants from 35.2 per 1,000 in 1980 to 20.4 per 1,000 in 1984 (68).

105.   Population growth is outpacing the capacity of a number of developing countries to provide for their economic and social well-being. The pressures thus generated are depleting natural resources faster than they can be regenerated, and reducing their productivity, and hence are undermining development.

106.   There is no simple correlation between population and the environment. Population, environment and development factors interact in different ways in different places. Not only the pace of development, but its content, location and the distribution of its benefits determine, in good measure, the state of the environment. These factors also influence the growth and distribution of population. Environmental resources provide the basis for development just as environmental factors constitute part of the improvement in the quality of life that development is meant to bring about. Similarly, the size of population, the rate of its growth and the pattern of its distribution influence the state of the environment, just as they condition the pace and composition of development.

107.   Population growth need not necessarily lower levels of living, impair the quality of life or cause environmental degradation. Global and historical assessments of the Earth's capacity and human ingenuity to produce goods and services have prompted some experts to project an optimistic outlook (69, 70). Growth of world population has, in the past, been accompanied by a steady increase in the world's capacity to provide for the necessities and amenities of human life. People have to be fed, clothed and provided for, and this is achieved by people themselves. In that process, they use and develop the resources of the environment. Yet, just as some patterns of development have improved the human environment, others have tended to degrade it, at times irreversibly.

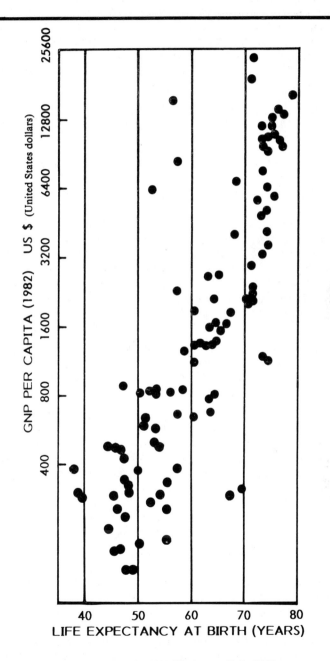

Figure 13.
The relationship between life expectancy at birth and GNP per capita in 1982

Source: World Bank, The World Bank Atlas 1985 (Washington D.C., 1985).

40

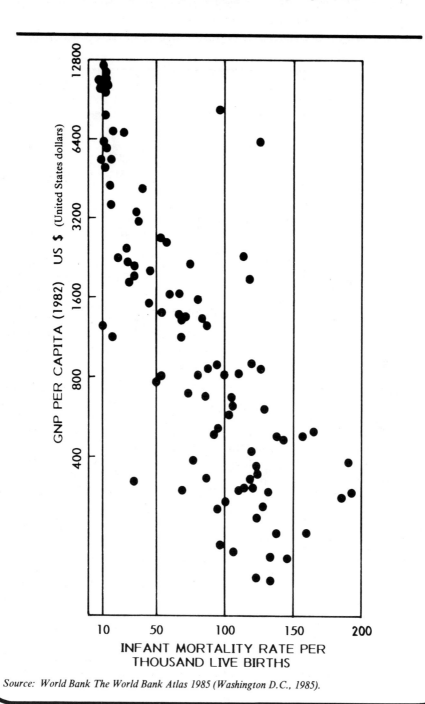

Figure 14.
The relationship between infact mortality and GNP per capita in 1982

GNP PER CAPITA (1982)   US $ (United States dollars)

INFANT MORTALITY RATE PER
THOUSAND LIVE BIRTHS

Source: World Bank The World Bank Atlas 1985 (Washington D.C., 1985).

108.   In a large number of countries, notably in Africa, rapid growth of population over the last decade has been accompanied by a steady decline in average levels of living, as reflected in per capita incomes. It has also been accompanied by a decline in the quality of life, as measured by indicators such as per capita availability of food and nutrition, drinking water and sanitation. Furthermore, the last decade has witnessed an increase in the number of people with inadequate or no access to essential services (such as health care) or amenities (such as shelter) in Africa, Asia and Latin America.

109.   On the other hand, even though, over some stretches of the decade, rates of economic growth appeared to be satisfactory in some developing countries, they did not necessarily bring about noticeable improvements in the levels of living of the majority of their peoples. Environmental conditions in rural as well as urban areas in many developing countries have deteriorated as their populations have grown. Generally speaking, the quantity and quality of their natural resources, which provide the foundation for sustained development, have steadily declined (67).

HUMAN SETTLEMENTS, TRANSPORT AND TOURISM

Human settlements

110.   Throughout the world, the single most frequent form of human settlement is the village. Cities and towns are far fewer than villages; they are more concentrated in the more developed regions of the world. In these regions, the proportion of population living in urban areas was 66 per cent in 1970 and has increased to 73 per cent in 1985. On the other hand, in the less developed regions, the proportion of population living in urban areas was 25 per cent in 1970 and reached 32 per cent in 1985. On a global basis, the percentage of people living in urban areas increased from 37 per cent in 1970 to 42 per cent in 1985 and is projected to reach more than 50 per cent by the year 2000.

111.   The pattern of urbanization in the less developed regions has been quite different from that which took place in more developed areas. Whereas urbanization in the industrialized countries took many decades, permitting a gradual emergence of economic, social and political institutions to deal with the problems of transformation, the process in developing countries is occurring far more rapidly, against a background of higher population growth and lower incomes. The transformation involves enormous members of people: between 1970 and 1980, the urban areas of developing regions absorbed about 320 million people; between 1980 and 2000, the increase is projected to be more than 1,000 million.

112.   Such a remarkable increase in urbanization in the developing countries has been accompanied by a rapid expansion of the number of very large cities. It was estimated that in 1975 there were 95 cities of more than one million inhabitants in the developed regions and 90 in the developing regions; a median projection of growth to the year 2000 showed 155 and 284 in both regions, respectively. In 1950, only one city in the less developed regions (greater Buenos Aires) had a population over 4 million. In 1960 there were 8 cities that had reached or exceeded that size, compared to 10 cities in the developed regions. In 1980, there were 22 such cities in the developing regions and only 16 in the developed regions. It has been estimated that by the year 2000, the developing regions will have about 61 cities with a population of or above 4 million, compared to about 25 in the developed regions. Eighteen cities in developing countries are expected to have more than 10 million inhabitants by that time.

113.   Rapid urbanization has been sustained by the combination of high rates of natural population increase and rural-to-urban migration. The relative contribution of each to urban population growth varies, but in the majority of cities natural increases are the primary contributing factor. However, the two sources are intertwined, for a large proportion of those leaving the countryside are in their reproductive years, and this may be partly responsible for the high rates of natural population increase in urban centres.

114.   The increasing concentration of people in urban centres has strained the capacity of most Governments to provide basic services. Illegal settlements, such as slums and squatter settlements, are common. In such areas people are usually deprived of access to the basic facilities of drinking water and waste disposal. They are frequently forced to use open water for washing, cleaning and the disposal of waste in unhygienic ways; and to live in makeshift shelters surrounded by accumulating domestic waste. Often, unhygienic living conditions in slums spread diseases, such as typhoid, cholera, malaria and hepatitis, through entire settlements.

115.   Low incomes and weak purchasing power are manifestations of the poverty that characterizes most families living in slums and squatter settlements. The cause of this poverty lies in the lack of sufficient opportunities for steady and gainful employment. The major problem for most families is underemployment and the resultant low, fluctuating incomes. Underemployment rates for slums and squatter settlements can reach more than 60 per cent (71). Despite the great variety of occupations cutting across all sectors of the urban economy, most slum and squatter-settlement residents work in the informal sector and in the lowest paying categories of work in the formal sector. Comparatively few are engaged in occupations requiring higher levels of skills and training.

116.   The economically precarious conditions of most slum and squatter-settlement residents trigger an increasing number of social hazards: an increase in the number of conflicts among residents of these settlements; an increase in the number of riots and the extent of crime and drug addiction (which in turn tends to increase the crime rate); and, ultimately, increasing mistrust and alienation between the regular urban dwellers and the slum-dwellers.

117.   People in the crowded squatter settlements in the developing areas are most prone to the effects of natural disasters (54). Recently, populations of this type have also been tragically affected by industrial accidents. In November 1984, a massive explosion at a liquefied petroleum gas storage facility in the crowded San Juanico neighbourhood of Mexico City killed 452 people, injured 4,248 and displaced 31,000. The blast illustrated the dangers inherent in a city where many of the 17 million inhabitants live on the doorstep of a variety of potentially dangerous installations. In December 1984, methyl isocyanate leaked from a pesticide plant on the outskirts of Bhopal, India, killing more than 2,500 of the people living in the slums nearby. More than 20,000 were seriously affected by the gas, and at least 200,000 people had to leave their homes to take temporary refuge elsehwere. Both disasters illustrate the lack of appropriate urban planning, which is a common feature in most developing countries, and the hazardous environments that have been created by rapid urbanization.

Transport

118.   The number of motor vehicles on the road in the world increased from about 246 million in 1970 to about 427 million in 1980 and reached 467 million in 1983 (1). The vast majority of motor vehicles were in OECD countries, accounting for 86.2 per cent of all vehicles in 1970 and for 76.2 per cent in 1983. The number of motor vehicles is, however, rapidly increasing in the developing countries, doubling from about 53 million in 1975 to about 111 million in 1983. The number increased at a much slower rate in OECD countries,

29 per cent fom 1975 to 1983. Passenger cars made up the bulk of motor vehicles on the road. It has been estimated that the average level of motorization is now about 75 cars per 1,000 inhabitants in the world as a whole—but reaches 540 in the United States, over 400 in Canada, Australia and New Zealand, 220 in Japan and from 200 to 400 in Europe (1). It has also been estimated that the world fleet of passenger cars will increase to about 700 million by the year 2000—one car for every eight people (72). Road freight has also increased in scale and efficiency. Modern diesel-powered lorries, often with trailers, are providing a dramatically increased level of community service, especially over short distances. The number of goods vehicles in the world increased from about 68 million in 1975 to about 99 million in 1983 (about 68 per cent of which were in OECD countries).

119.   Other kinds of transport also grew over the past decade. The total volume of international seaborne trade reached 3,320 million tons in 1984, an increase of 6.7 per cent over 1983. Tanker cargoes in 1984 (1,427 million tons) showed a slight increase over 1983, but were still 23.7 per cent less than in 1980. Dry cargo, however, reached record volumes in 1984 (1,893 million tons) with both main bulk commodities and other dry cargo increasing by more than 10.6 per cent over 1983 (73). Over the past decade there have been also increases in air traffic and rail transport, and pipelines are now transporting coal, gas, oil and other bulk materials over longer distances.

120.   The expansion of transport in the world, especially in developing countries has obviously consumed much land. The length of motorways in the OECD countries increased from 73,000 km in 1970 to 108,000 km in 1980 (an increase of 48 per cent) and reached 114,000 km in 1983, while total road length rose from 11.7 million km in 1970 to 12.5 million km in 1983 (1). Road development programmes have been scaled down, and the road networks in OECD countries have been expanding at a much slower rate than in the past. This slow-down has been attributed to economic and, in part, to environmental causes, but it is also due to the fact that most OECD countries have already established most of the necessary infrastructure and have reached the level of "saturation". The situation is different in developing countries, where there is need for additional roads of all kinds. The pace of construction has, however, been slow for economic reasons, existing roads are not adequately maintained and in most countries their condition has deteriorated.

121.   In both developed and developing countries, the ever increasing number of motor vehicles on the roads since the 1950s has resulted in an upsurge of traffic accidents, which have taken on the characteristics of an epidemic. It has been estimated that about 300,000 people are killed each year in traffic accidents and that several millions are injured (74). While fatality rates probably exceed 50 per 100 million vehicle-kilometres in some developing countries (e.g. Lesotho and Sierra Leone), they have been reduced to less than 5 per 100 million vehicle-kilometres in developed countries. Following the road safety measures introduced in most European countries since 1973 (speed limits, compulsory seat belts, crash helmets, etc) the numbers of killed and injured dropped sharply despite the increase in the number of cars in use (see figure 15). In many congested cities in the developing countries, such as Caracas, Bangkok and Cairo, pressure for driving and parking space has meant encroachment on the pavements to the extent that space for pedestrians barely exists, and walking and cycling have become dangerous and unpleasant.

122.   Transport is a great consumer of energy. The efficiency of energy utilization varies considerably. Railroads and waterways, for example, are more efficient than aircraft or automobiles. The latter are the least efficient, and they account for the bulk of energy consumption in the transport sector. Private cars consume about 7 per cent of the world's commercial energy, or 17 per cent of oil used each year (75). The United States, in fact, uses 10 per cent of the world's oil output as gasoline for motor cars and light trucks. Substantial energy savings can be made in the transportation system by improving engineering, by improving load factors on existing modes, by switching increasing volumes of traffic to

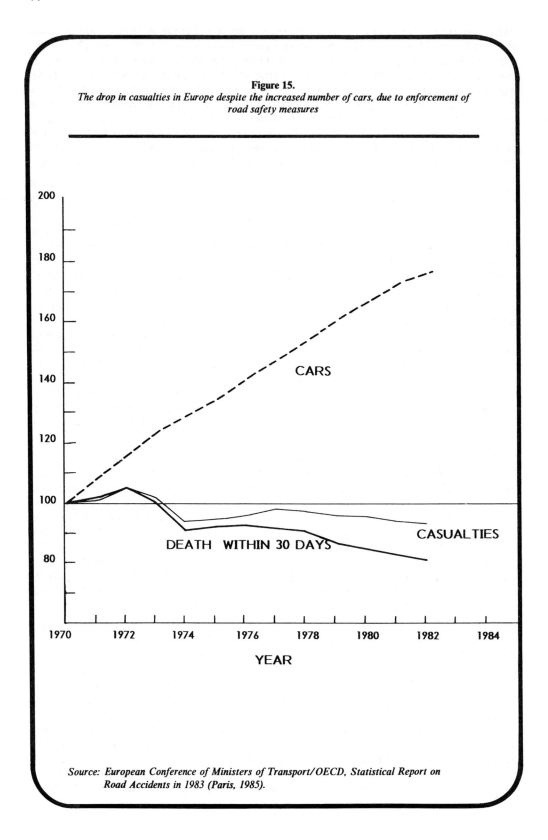

Figure 15.
The drop in casualties in Europe despite the increased number of cars, due to enforcement of road safety measures

CARS

DEATH WITHIN 30 DAYS

CASUALTIES

YEAR

Source: European Conference of Ministers of Transport/OECD, Statistical Report on Road Accidents in 1983 (Paris, 1985).

more efficient modes, and, more importantly, by changing transport habits. Fuel economy around the world averages about 21 miles per gallon (8.9 km per litre), though it varies widely (the United States automobile fleet has the highest rate of oil consumption). New cars have a fuel economy of up to 32 miles per gallon and several manufacturers have produced prototype cars that obtain up to 93 miles per gallon (75). The predominant use of light automobiles in some countries and the switch to buses and fixed rail transport systems in intra-city travel has led to considerable energy savings (75, 76). Conservation efforts in the transport sector often bring other benefits. For example, the lowering of highway speed limits in the United States and other countries (which was intended to increase fuel efficiency) had the additional benefit of increasing automobile tyre life and, more importantly, reducing highway accidents and deaths.

123.   The most familiar environmental impacts of road transport are those from air pollution. Petrol-burning vehicles emit carbon monoxide, hydrocarbons, oxides of nitrogen, particulates and trace compounds. In confined spaces (like tunnels or very narrow streets) carbon monoxide concentrations can rise to levels hazardous to health, especially to people with heart or lung weakness. Oxides of nitrogen and hydrocarbons, on the other hand, are not directly toxic, but interact in the presence of sunlight to produce an oxidant smog which irritates the eyes and lungs and damages sensitive plants. Most OECD countries have introduced emission standards for new motor vehicles (especially standards for carbon monoxide, hydrocarbons and nitrogen oxides). In most European countries, the lead content of petrol has been reduced to levels between 0.15 and 0.40 grams per litre. Unleaded petrol has been introduced in some countries, for example, in Switzerland, and steps are being taken to introduce it in other countries (1). It is widely available in the Federal Republic of Germany, and there are several hundred outlets in the United Kingdom, France and Italy. Recent studies have shown that trace metals are more highly concentrated on vegetation and soil near highways than on crops from sites farther away (77, 78). The discharge of used motor oils in the environment poses public health problems because such oils contain high quantities of polycyclic aromatic hydrocarbons which are known to be carcinogenic (79).

124.   More and more automobiles and light-duty trucks are likely to be equipped with diesel engines in the future because they have higher fuel efficiencies than gasoline engines and because diesel fuel traditionally has cost less than gasoline. Current diesel-powered vehicles emit more visible smoke and odours than gasoline-powered vehicles, and this has led to concern about their possible effect on human health and the environment. Diesel vehicles emit 30-50 times more particulate matter than a comparable gasoline vehicle (80). Diesel exhaust particles consist of chain aggregates of carbon microspheres coated with a variety of organic compounds that comprise between 15 and 65 per cent of the total particle mass. Several hundred organic compounds have been identified in solvent extracts of diesel exhaust particles, many of which are known to be carcinogenic.

125.   Of all present-day sources of noise, the noise from transportation—above all that from road vehicles is the most diffused. In many countries it is the source that creates the greatest problems. Everywhere it is growing in intensity, spreading to areas until now unaffected, reaching ever further into the night hours and creating as much concern as any other type of pollution. Recent data show that about 110 million people are exposed to road traffic noise levels in excess of 65 dBA in OECD countries (1). For aircraft noise, about 0.5 per cent of the population in the European countries and Japan are exposed to noise levels in excess of 65 dBA, whereas the proportion of the population affected in the United States is 2 per cent, or some 5 million people. However, in so many countries a major source of noise pollution is neighbourhood noise, especially noise accentuated by poor standards of insulation and construction in modern dwellings. Overall, 16 per cent of the population of OECD countries—approximately 130 million people—are exposed to noise levels in excess

of 65 dBA. It is recognized in many countries that the percentage of population living in these "grey" areas, that is those exposed to noise levels between 55 and 65 dBA, is increasing and therefore noise has become a more significant problem than it was thought to be few years ago. Many countries have adopted regulations to control maximum permissible noise levels for the different categories of motor vehicles. However, the problem still remains (even increasing in magnitude in several urban centres in developing countries), and more efforts are required to reduce the exposure to noise from traffic.

Tourism

126.   Tourism, with its different categories—international, interregional and domestic— has become a major industry dependent on the continued availability of a number of generally renewable resources. International tourism has grown rapidly from 180 million arrivals in 1971 to 286 million in 1980 to about 350 million in 1985. International tourist receipts rose fivefold in 10 years, from 18,200 million in 1970 to 92,000 million in 1980. Receipts in 1985 were about 120,000 million.

127.   Various analyses of the economic, cultural, social and environmental aspects of tourism (37, 81, 82) reveal a picture of increasing activity with both negative and positive impacts. A key principle advocated recently by those who seek a balance between tourism and the environment is that the type and scale of tourist development and activity should be related to the carrying capacity of tourist resources (83-88). Such an idea has an obvious relevance to, for example, the airlines or water supply systems serving a particular tourist resort. However, the principle applies equally to the social system and the physical or cultural resources that may form the basic attraction to the tourist. The social system—the population and its workforce—can absorb and serve only a certain number of tourists before strains begin to appear. The physical resources, such as beaches, ski slopes or game reserves, may take a certain load of tourist activity, but show signs of deterioration if that load is exceeded. From 1972 to 1984, the numbers of visitors to parks continued to increase in most countries, such as the United States, Australia, Mexico, Thailand and Turkey. Other countries have had relatively stable or mildly fluctuating numbers in more recent years, as was the case with the Federal Republic of Germany, Brazil and Kenya. Assessment of carrying capacity, and the balancing of levels of tourist development and activity with that capacity, are therefore a crucial means of preventing environmental damage, protecting resources and securing the continuance of tourism itself on a "sustained yield" basis.

AGRICULTURE AND FOOD PRODUCTION

Current trends in food production

128.   Agricultural output and food production has increased only slightly in the period 1980-1985; the total production of cereals in the world increased from 1,568 million tons in 1980 to 1,837 million tons in 1985; root crops increased from 536 million to 585 million tons; fruits from 290 million to 300 million tons; meat from 132 million to 148 million tons; milk from 466 million to 508 million tons; and fishery products from 72 million to 84 million tons (50, 89). On a per capita production basis, and in spite of some fluctuations, there has been a slight increase in cereals production but a drop in root crops since 1970. The per capita production of fruits, meat, milk and fishery products has remained nearly stable since 1970.

129.   World-wide, the annual rate of growth of agricultural output was 3.1 per cent in the 1950s, 2.5 per cent in the 1960s, and 2.3 per cent in the period 1971-1984 (90, 91). Growth in world food production slowed in 1985 (2.1 per cent) to less than half the rate achieved in 1984 (4.7 per cent) and less than the average for the period 1980-1985 (2.6 per cent) (50). There was a sharp deceleration in growth in developed countries (from 6.5 per cent in 1984 to 0.8 per cent in 1985), while in developing countries growth was maintained at the 1984 rate of increase (3.0 per cent), but below the average for the period 1980-1985 (3.6 per cent). However, substantial regional differences exist. There was an acceleration of growth in agricultural output in South-East Asia from 2.9 per cent per year in the 1960s to 3.8 per cent per year in the 1970s; in Latin America there was a slight increase, from 2.9 per cent to 3.0 per cent; but in Africa the rate of growth declined from 3.0 per cent per year in the 1960s to 1.2 per cent per year since 1971 (91). As can be seen from figure 16, the per capita grain production in Africa dropped markedly below subsistence level in the last ten years.

130.   Although the total calorie and protein content of today's food production is more than twice the minimum requirement of the world population, famine and malnutrition remain widespread. The situation has been created and aggravated by a combination of social, economic, environmental and political factors, ranging from the inequitable access to resources and products to the often primitive contidions of production and processing of agricultural output in many areas. Precise estimates of the incidence of chronic malnutrition in developing countries are not possible, but by any account the problem is vast. A recent estimate by the World Bank puts the number somewhere between 340 million and 730 million people (91). If present trends continue, more than 10 per cent of the world population will remain seriously undernourished by the year 2000, unless agricultural output is increased in developing countries. FAO pointed out in 1981 that a world population of more than 6 billion in the year 2000 will require a level of agricultural output some 50 to 60 per cent higher than in 1980. Demand for food and agricultural products in developing countries will double.

Increasing agricultural output

131.   There are two main approaches to the task of raising agricultural output: increasing the area of cultivated land, and increasing the yield per unit of land.

132.   The total area of potential arable land in the world is about 3,200 million hectares, about 46 per cent of which (1,500 million hectares) is already under cultivation. It has been said that very large areas of new land could be brought under cultivation, but unused arable land is not always available to people who need it most, and opening up new areas remains an expensive means of increasing agricultural production. FAO estimates that about 10 to 15 per cent of unused arable land (170 million to 255 million hectares) might be cultivated by the year 2000 (90). Other estimates are 100 million hectares and 300 million hectares.

133.   The alternative to increasing the area under cultivation is to use existing land more efficiently. Efforts to do so have been successful: productivity gains have been achieved largely by improving the availability and reliability of irrigation and increasing the use of high-yield varieties (HYVs) of grain and modern agricultural management. It has been estimated that about 55 million hectares (35 per cent of cultivated land in the developing countries) are planted to HYVs of wheat and rice (94). The new wheats were largely responsible for India's increase in wheat production from 11.4 million tons in 1964 to 35 million in 1980. Similarly, rice production in Indonesia rose from 12.2 million tons in 1970 to over 22 million in 1981 (94). In developing countries, cereal yields rose by 2 per cent a year between 1961 and 1980; yields of wheat varieties by 2.7 per cent; yields of sorghum by 2.4 per cent. Although rice yields increased by only 1.6 per cent a year in developing countries as a whole, they rose by more than 3 per cent a year in Indonesia and the Philippines, which were best suited to the new varieties (90).

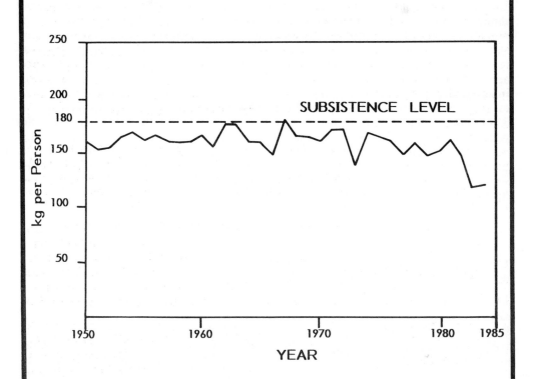

Figure 16.
Per capita grain production in Africa

*Source: L.R. Brown and E.C. Wolf, "Soil erosion: quiet crisis", Worldwatch paper No. 60
(Washington D.C., Worldwatch Institute, 1984)*

134.   The "green revolution" technological packages require HYVs of seeds and high inputs of water, fertilizers and pesticides. Over the world as a whole, 1,300 billion cubic metres of water are used for irrigation every year, but for this, 3,000 billion cubic metres have to be withdrawn. In other words, 57 per cent of total water withdrawn is lost in the process of storage and transport (95). Growth in the use of water for irrigation has been linked to two factors: the expansion of the area under irrigation (from 163 million hectares in 1968 to 213 million in 1981 and, according to some estimates (38), to about 258 million hectares in 1984 and 271 million in 1985) and the extent to which techniques of water application and land management have allowed economies in the amount of water used.

135.   The increased application of chemical fertilizers supplying plant nutrients (nitrogen, phosphorus and potassium) is an essential component of modern agriculture. World consumption of chemical fertilizers rose markedly in the past decade. For nitrogen fertilizers, use increased from 32 million tons of nitrogen in 1971 to 61 million tons in 1983; for phosphates, from 21 million tons of phosphorus pentoxide to 31 million tons; and for potash, from 16 million tons of potassium oxide to 24 million tons (89). The rate of application of fertilizers to land increased markedly with the introduction of HYVs of seeds. The use of fertilizers varies widely from one country to another: in India, the figure is 36 Kg/ha; in Hungary, 233 kg/ha; in the United States, 98 kg/ha; in Japan, 412 kg/ha (96). World-wide, the consumption of fertilizers increased from 62 kg/ha in the period 1974-1976 to 80 kg/ha in 1981-1983 (96). It has been estimated that the future annual rate of growth of fertilizer use in the world will be about 8 per cent, with agricultural production doubling between 1980 and 2000.

136.   Recent studies have shown that only about 50 per cent of the fertilizer is used by crops; the remainder is lost from the soil with no benefit to the crop (97). Chief among the environmental problems of increased fertilizer use, are the contributions of phosphate and nitrogen fertilizers to eutrophication of surface waters, and the excessive concentration of nitrogen compounds, especially in ground water (see paras. 43-49 above).

137.   World sales of pesticides (figure 17) totalled 5.5 billion in 1975 and about US$28 billion in 1985 (1, 98). This represents about a 18 per cent annual increase in sales, at 1977 United States dollar prices. About 80 per cent of the pesticides used in the world are used in the developed countries. It has been estimated that if agricultural output is to be doubled between 1980 and 2000, the consumption of pesticides in the developed countries will have to grow at a rate of 2-4 per cent per year, with a rate of 7-8 per cent in the developing regions (98).

138.   The amount of pesticide impinging on target pests is generally an extremely small percentage of the amount applied. Often less than 0.1 per cent of pesticides applied to crops actually reaches target pests (99). Thus, over 99 per cent moves into ecosystems to contaminate the land, water and air. Pesticide residues are a common cause of poisoning both in the field and in the home and a widespread but largely unassessed source of chronic professional exposure. They also can expose people at low levels through ingestion of food contaminated at concentrations far below those giving rise to overt toxic symptoms. Concentrations of persistent organochlorine compounds in food and dietary intakes of contaminants are measured in a number of countries. At the international level, the ongoing FAO/WHO/UNEP joint food contamination monitoring programme receives data on contaminants in the food and diet from 22 participating countries. Organochlorine residue concentrations in terrestrial, freshwater and marine wildlife have been available through some national monitoring programmes, especially in OECD countries. DDT complex levels in the fat of cow's milk showed a marked decline in Japan and the Netherlands during the 1970s, and a similar trend is observed in Japanese and United States finfish. Those of aldrin and dieldrin have been falling consistently in both cow's and human milk in Japan, the Netherlands and Switzerland.

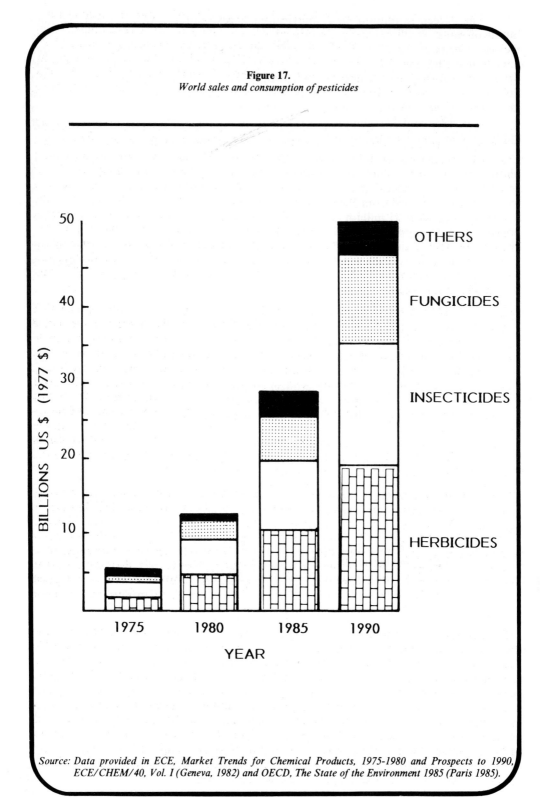

Figure 17.
World sales and consumption of pesticides

Source: Data provided in ECE, Market Trends for Chemical Products, 1975-1980 and Prospects to 1990, ECE/CHEM/40, Vol. 1 (Geneva, 1982) and OECD, The State of the Environment 1985 (Paris 1985).

139.   The WHO, in co-operation with UNEP established in 1973 an environmental health criteria programme which aims at the evaluation of the effects of chemicals on human health and the quality of the environment. In 1980, the programme was incorporated into the International Programme on Chemical Safety (IPCS). Within the framework of this Programme, environmental health criteria have been published for a number of pesticides, for example, for DDT, heptachlor, paraquat, diquat, endosulfan, quintozene, technazene, chlordecone and mirex.

140.   The repeated application of pesticides to a pest population can result in the selection of individuals which can tolerate doses of the pesticide higher than that required to kill the majority. The individual members of "resistant strains" can breed and thus produce resistant populations. Although resistance to pesticides has been known since 1911, it has occured at a greatly accelerated pace since 1947 as a result of the large-scale introduction and application of synthetic pesticides (101-102). Figure 18 illustrates the growth in the number of pesticide resistant arthropods and new insecticides introduced in the period from 1938-1980. The danger of the situation is that there is reason to suppose that all pests are likely to be able to develop resistance to all types of chemical pesticide in time, given appropriate selection pressure. This could seriously and adversely affect the efficiency and economy of pest control operations on a global scale, with corresponding grave effects on both world health and world food production.

141.   The best alternative approach, especially in the long-term, would be one that altogether avoids, or reduces the need for, the use of pesticides. There are five alternative approaches to chemical pest control: environmental control; genetic and sterile male technique; biological control; behavioural control; and resistance breeding. However, the best alternative that has attracted increased attention is "integrated pest management", which seeks to develop an approach to pest control based on the integration of all control techniques relevant to the specific pest/host complex under consideration. While this system has been considerably developed, both in theory and in practice, there are difficulties in its application. One major obstacle is that the common subsidies on pesticides in the developing countries (total subsidies ranges from 15 per cent of what the total retail cost would be without subsidy to as high as 80-90 per cent) undermine efforts to promote the most cost-effective methods of integrated pest management (103).

142.   In spite of the great achievements in agriculture through the introduction of cultivars suited to specific environments and production practices, the extensive use of HYVs of seeds is expected to lead to a marked decrease in genetic diversity. This causes two kinds of problems. First, the uniformity of the genetic background of HYVs opens up the possibility that a new disease or pest to which they are not resistant could sweep through an entire area, causing a large crop failure. The second problem is that the reserves of genetic diversity that allow breeders to produce varieties resistant to new diseases and other stresses are being lost as farmers in the developing countries, who grew many varieties and thus were a major source of genetic variability, switch to HYVs.

143.   Efforts are now under way to apply genetic engineering technologies to specific agricultural problems. If genetic engineering techniques can be mastered, it will be possible to make use of them in the design of plants that are hardier, more nutritious or less expensive to produce, or offer high yields. Other possibilities include plants that can thrive in marginal conditions, on soils that are very salty, very acidic, very wet or very dry (104—109). The successful application of genetic engineering to plants will require fundamental breakthroughs in the understanding of gene expression and regulation, as well as increased knowledge of plant physiology, biochemistry, development and metabolism. It is too early to assess with accuracy either the potential or the limitations of genetic engineering as far as crop improvement is concerned. At this stage, gene transfer is not expected to have a significant effect on agricultural production practices until the late 1990s.

52

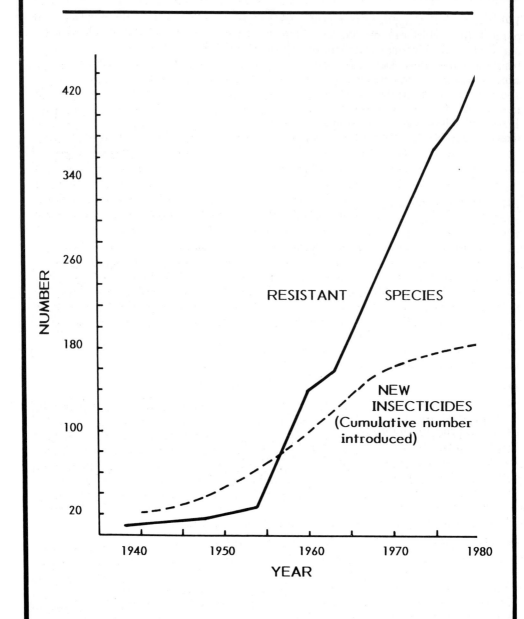

Figure 18.
Resistant species of arthropods and new insecticides introduced, 1938-1980

Source: Adapted from D. Bull, Pesticides and the Third World— A Growing Problem (London, Oxfam, 1982)

144.   Genetic engineering can affect not only what crops can be grown, but where and how they are grown. It usually acts in conjunction with other biological and mechanical innovations, the deployment of which is governed by social, economic, environmental and political factors. Although our knowledge of the environmental consequences of plant genetic engineering is in its infancy, researchers and the public are becoming increasingly concerned about the safety of the new technology (110—113). One cause for such concern is the risk posed by the release of novel organisms into the environment. The introduction of any species into an ecosystem it does not normally inhabit can produce unexpected problems. Guiding or perhaps accelerating the course of evolution can lead to changes which disrupt an ecosystem and, hence, may undermine reverence for life.

145.   The introduction of genetically engineered plants, like the introduction of cultivars through normal plant breeding, should have beneficial environmental effects—for example, the reduction of chemical fertilizer and pesticide use, increased tolerance to salt and drought, and so on. However, if drought tolerance leads to the expansion of dryland cropping into ever-drier regions where rainfall variations from year to year are extreme, increased wind and water erosion could result in severe soil degradation during dry years. The introduction of salt-tolerant species could prompt increased use of saline water for irrigation, with the subsequent contamination of shallow ground water and increased salinization of soils. This in turn would narrow the choice of crops for cultivation in rotation. Increased tolerance to herbicides could make it difficult to eradicate crop plants that have become weeds. So with all these new developments strict care is required to ensure that in solving one problem, we are not creating much more difficult ones.

146.   Although more than 20,000 edible plants are known, and perhaps 3,000 have been used by mankind at one time or another in history, a mere handful of crops now dominate the world's food supply (see figure 19). To help feed, clothe, and house an increasing population, to make marginal lands more productive, and to reforest the devastated tropics, we need a revitalized world-wide investigation of little-known plant species. Such an effort would expand our agricultural resource base and ease our dangerous dependence on such a small number of crops.

Fish Production

147.   Fish is one of the most widely distributed food commodities in the world. It presently contributes about 6 per cent of the total protein supplies and, taking into account the indirect contribution of fishmeal fed to animals, about 24 per cent of the world's animal protein supplies (89). For many developing countries, fish is an indispensable item of daily diets. About 60 per cent of the population of the developing world derive 40 per cent or more of their total annual protein supplies from fish. Fish and fish products are not only highly nutritious, with protein content varying between 15 and 20 per cent but their biochemistry and amino-acid characteristics make them particularly efficient in supplementing the cereal and tuber diets widely consumed in Asia and Africa.

148.   The total world fish production reached 84 million tons in 1985 (see paragraphs 66-67 above). The total world aquaculture production has been estimated at about 9 million tons (115), consisting mainly of finfish, shellfish and seaweed. Since fish is grown for home consumption in backyard ponds in many developing countries (especially in Asian countries), this figure does not include such "non-commercial" production which is difficult to account for. At present aquaculture production constitutes about 8-9 per cent of total world fish production and is developing continuously and at a rapid rate (5-7 per cent per year), particularly in South-East Asia, Japan, Europe and North America (1, 115). It is expected that aquaculture production will reach 20 million tons by the year 2000, mainly from fresh water ponds.

54

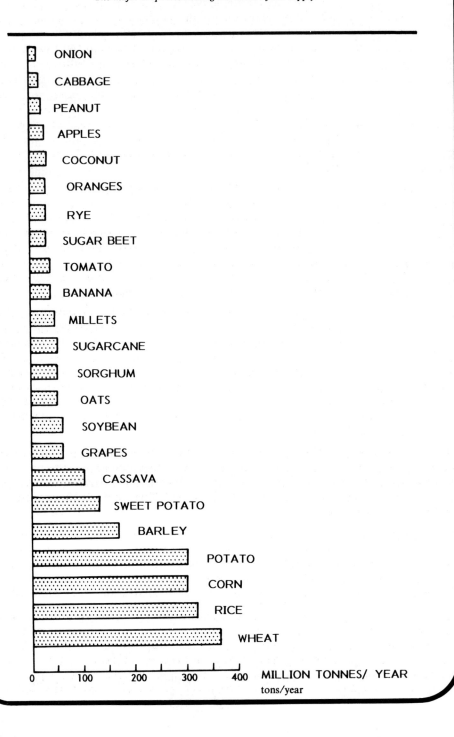

Figure 19.
The major crops dominating the world's food supply

ONION
CABBAGE
PEANUT
APPLES
COCONUT
ORANGES
RYE
SUGAR BEET
TOMATO
BANANA
MILLETS
SUGARCANE
SORGHUM
OATS
SOYBEAN
GRAPES
CASSAVA
SWEET POTATO
BARLEY
POTATO
CORN
RICE
WHEAT

0   100   200   300   400   MILLION TONNES/ YEAR
tons/year

INDUSTRIAL DEVELOPMENT

Industry and the environment

149.   The industrial sector constitutes a major component of the economy in most countries. It plays a major role in the economic development of many countries and in the economic welfare of their citizens. It provides employment for a large proportion of the population and supplies the material goods they consume. The contribution of industry to the gross domestic product (GDP) of low-income economies has increased from 28 per cent in 1965 to 35 per cent in 1984. For middle-income economies the contribution increased from 31 per cent in 1965 to 37 per cent in 1984. On the other hand, in industrial market economies, the contribution of industry to GDP decreased from 39 per cent in 1965 to 35 per cent in 1984 (91). This can be attributed to the general downturn and stagnation in industrial output in these countries since 1979. As a matter of fact the period 1979-1984 was characterized by the decline in OECD of traditional industries such as textiles, leather, iron and steel and petrochemicals (1, 116).

150.   One of the important trends over the period 1979-1985 was the emergence of many innovations and scientific advances in some industries in the developed countries. The application of new technologies, particularly in areas such as robotics, automation, micro-electronics, information technology and biotechnology, has provided the basis for and driving force behind the development of new high technology industries and also for the modernization of existing production processes in traditional industries such as textiles and pulp and paper. Of particular interest, has been the growth in the pollution control industry, which is currently estimated to employ about 1.5 million people in Europe (1).

151.   The industrial sector includes a large number of diverse activities involving the extraction and processing, including the synthesis, of various materials and their use in the manufacture of products. Consequently, there is also a wide range of diverse resource and environmental impacts created by this sector. Industrial processes generate different airborne emissions, water effluents, and solid wastes that can affect human health and environment in many ways. The risks of industrial accidents and explosions present a serious potential environmental danger in the form of clouds of toxic gases and the contamination of water courses and a disposal problem for the contaminated wastes resulting from the clean-up operations.

152.   The environmental impacts of chemical products have been of particular concern to policy makers and the general public over the last ten years. According to recent estimates, about 9 million chemicals are known (117), some 80,000 organic and inorganic compounds are in commercial production, and a further 1,000 to 2,000 new chemicals currently appear on the market every year.

153.   Although a vast amount of scientific information is available on the short-term effects of well known chemicals hazardous to human health or animal species, it is still not known what happens if people are exposed to these or other chemicals at very low concentrations over a period of 20 or 30 years. Effects may appear a long time after exposure to either a large dose over a short period, or a relatively small dose over an extended period.

154.   The immediate impacts on human health and the environment resulting from an accident in an industrial plant, including long-term effects, are a matter of concern. The release of dioxin after an explosion at a chemical plant in Seveso, Italy, in 1976, the explosion of a huge liquefied petroleum tank in Mexico in 1984, the major accident at a chemical plant in Bhopal, India, in December 1984, and the explosion of a depot in Sandoz Company in Switzerland, which spilled over 10 tons of toxic chemicals in the Rhine river in

November 1986 are examples of serious incidents that can occur and that cause genuine concern for the safety of man and the environment. UNEP is in the process of consultation with governments, relevant members of the United Nations system and industry to conclude international agreements on notification of industrial accidents and on mutual assistance in case of industrial accidents of this type.

155. A number of administrative and technical steps have recently been taken to prevent such accidents and mitigate their consequences. One example is the European Economic Community's directive on the major hazards of certain industrial activities (the "Seveso" directive). The directive obliges manufacturers within the Community to identify potential danger areas in the manufacturing process and to take all necessary measures to prevent major accidents as well as to limit their consequences, should they occur, for man and the environment. A major recommendation of the World Industry Conference on Environmental Management, held in Versailles, in November 1984, was that, in order to strengthen the anticipatory and preventive approach to environmental management within industry, each line manager from the chief executive down should also think of himself or herself as an environmental manager. Clear accountability for environmental performance should accompany managerial responsibility in each case.

156. Less attention has, however, hitherto been paid to routine emissions of small amounts of toxic chemicals as part of normal plant operations or as a result of minor accidents. To illustrate the magnitude of these releases, the United States National Response Centre received in the period between January 1983 and March 1985 more than 24,000 notifications of accidental releases. These included releases from both stationary sources such as chemical plants and mobile sources such as trucks. The United States Environmental Protection Agency estimates that approximately 2,000 potentially cancer-causing or toxic chemicals are likely to get into the air as a result of such releases (118).

157. A number of industrialized countries have enacted legislation in attempts to "control" industrial chemicals prior to marketing, in order to protect man and the environment by ensuring their proper handling and use. However, the task has been complex and slow because the tools necessary to evaluate chemical effects, especially long-term toxicology and ecotoxicology, are not sufficiently developed for the task. Assessment of risk to human populations based on data from laboratory animals remains a controversial issue, and many uncertainties remain regarding the methods used to determine the potential threat to the environment from chemicals.

158. Unlike developed countries, most developing countries have no toxic chemical control laws, nor the technical or institutional capability for implementing such laws. During recent years, several cases have come to light where products banned or severely restricted in the industrialized countries were sold to, or "dumped" on, the developing countries. Developing countries have been very concerned over this situation. In 1984, the UNEP Governing Council adopted a Provisional Notification Scheme for Banned and Severely Restricted Chemicals. Under the Scheme, the competent national authorities of exporting countries inform importing countries of national bans or restrictions on chemicals which are traded internationally. In addition, the United Nations has issued a list of products whose consumption and/or sale have been banned, withdrawn, severely restricted, or, in the case of pharmaceuticals, not approved by Governments. Some 500 products are already included in this list.

Hazardous waste

159. There is as yet, no universal definition of hazardous waste. According to the World Health Organization, it is a waste that "has physical, chemical or biological characteristics which require special handling and disposal procedures to avoid risk to health and/or other adverse environmental effects" (119).

160.   Estimates of the quantities of hazardous waste generated by industry vary widely, depending on the definition of hazardous waste used. It is estimated that OECD countries generate about 300 million tons of hazardous wastes annually, of which 264 million are from the United States (1). More than 10 per cent of the waste generated in OECD countries is transported across national frontiers for disposal. In 1983, about 2.2 million tons of hazardous waste crossed the national frontiers of the European member States of OECD on the way to treatment, storage and/or disposal. Cross-frontier traffic in such wastes in the European members of OECD is likely to involve between 20,000 and 30,000 border crossings annually. For North America, available data suggest about 5,000 annual border crossings for all hazardous wastes (1).

161.   The disposal of hazardous waste has become a difficult and controversial problem in waste management. In many cases the present methods for the disposal are not so reliable as to preclude any risk to man and the environment. In many countries no data, or only incomplete data, are available at the national level on amounts of hazardous wastes generated or on the disposal techniques used by producers. Over 75 per cent of hazardous waste generated by industries in OECD countries is disposed of on land, including landfills, deep-well injection and underground disposal. Wastes may be disposed of in bulk or stored in drums, barrels or tanks.

162.   A very severe problem in many countries is that of waste that was disposed of in thousands of unsatisfactory pre-existing landfill sites. Many such sites have been discovered during the last few years: for example, in Denmark, 3,200 abandoned sites have been found, 500 of them containing chemical waste, while, in the Netherlands, there are 4,000 abandoned sites and 350 require immediate remedial action (1). In the United States concern has been focused on the health effects of chemical waste in over 20,000 uncontrolled sites—many of which are abandoned, covered over, or even forgotten—that contain chemicals with enormous diversity of physical and chemical characteristics. The Comprehensive Environmental Response, Compensation and Liability Act (the Superfund Act) was passed in December 1980 to address these sites. As of March 1986, the United States Environmental Protection Agency had placed 842 sites on its national priority list for remedial attention. Under the Superfund Act, $1.6 billion have been earmarked for the remedial operations (1, 120).

163.   Laws controlling the disposal of hazardous wastes are now in effect in most developed countries. The immediate need is to make sure that they are enforced in a cost-effective and environmentally sound way. As the controls have tightened in many developing countries, chemical industries have had to pay more for getting rid of their wastes. Some have been tempted to avoid these extra costs by moving their operations or exporting their wastes to countries where the laws are less strict, or less strictly enforced. These countries could well become international dustbins, and end up with the same sort of problems that brought the strict legislation in the first place. There have even been a few cases where companies have shipped waste to another country, ostensibly for storage, and then abandoned it (121). Waste from the Netherlands ended up in the United Kingdom in this way, and wastes from the United States have been stored in a warehouse in Mexico (121). Recently, dioxin-containing waste from Seveso, Italy, disappeared during transfrontier transport and was finally found to be inadequately stored in an abandoned slaughterhouse in France. Developing countries would be particularly vulnerable to such pollution exports.

Cleaner technologies

164.   Recent technological advances present considerable potential for the development of cleaner technologies that reduce industry's emission of pollutants and use of energy. This includes developments in the following areas: environmental sensors to facilitate the

monitoring of pollution levels; information processing technology that can help improve the dissemination of information on subjects such as cleaner technologies; advances in biotechnology that have led to improvements in the effectiveness and efficiency of treating industrial effluents; and developments in micro-electronics that enable greater control over production processes and hence increased in-plant recycling of waste streams and reduced product losses, raw material consumption and pollutant emission; in addition, the possibilities for the recycling and re-use of industrial wastes in other industries or in special recycling industries are growing. For example, in Europe glass recycling has grown from about 1.3 million tons in 1979 to about 2.7 million in 1984. Recycling of aluminium cans in the USA increased from 24,000 tons in 1972 to 510,000 tons in 1982. In Bulgaria, the introduction of low- and non-waste technologies helped reduce the discharge of industrial wastes by about 5.5 million tons annually (4). Increasing use is made of wastes from the chemical, pharmaceutical and food-processing industries and from mining. In the German Democratic Republic, about 30 million tons of industrial wastes are recycled each year (39) providing 12 per cent of raw material required for industry. In Hungary, about 22.5 million tons of industrial wastes were generated in 1985; about 6.5 million tons of these were recycled (5). Scrap and paper recycling has also grown in several countries.

165.   These cleaner technologies achieve considerable reductions in the consumption of energy and raw materials by firms and in their discharges of pollutants. For example, a new closed ferrosilicon furnace in Norway achieves a higher yield, requires less energy and raw materials and generates less air pollution emissions. These new technologies are economically profitable in their own right in some cases, and are undertaken for a combination of economic and environmental reasons. In other cases, the new technologies are more effective and efficient than alternative conventional treatment techniques and are undertaken to enable the firm concerned to comply with environmental regulations more efficiently.

166.   While technological advances offer considerable potential for environmental improvement, some technological developments coupled with changes in the structure of industry and in the types of materials used in production processes are leading to the emergence of new types of pollution problems, including a shift from traditional pollutants to more complex toxic pollutants such as heavy metals, toxic air and water pollutants and hazardous wastes.

ENERGY

167.   The world commercial energy consumption has increased more than threefold over the past three decades. In 1970, total consumption was about 5,000 million tons of oil equivalent (t.o.e.); in 1980, the figure was about 7,000 million t.o.e. and in 1985, it reached 7,400 million t.o.e. (figure 20). In 1985, oil accounted for about 40 per cent of world commercial energy consumption, whereas it had accounted for about 47 per cent in 1973.

168.   Consumption of the world's commercial energy resources is heavily concentrated in the developed regions—the industrial market economies and the centrally-planned economies. These regions, with about 30 per cent of the total world population, account for about 85 per cent of the total world consumption of commercial energy; the other 70 per cent of the population, comprising the developing countries consume about 15 per cent (see figure 20). The per capita commercial energy consumption in the OECD countries is about nine times that in the developing countries (see figure 21).

169.   Several studies have been made to estimate future energy demand in the world (38, 122). Estimates vary from 9,500 million t.o.e. to 12,000 million t.o.e. by the year 2000. Wider variations exist in longer-term forecasts; the maximum estimate reaches 39,000 million t.o.e.

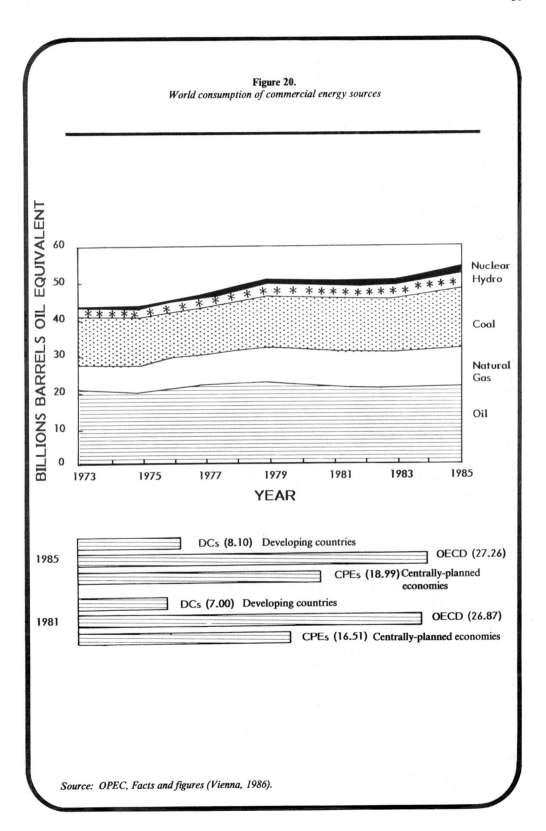

Figure 20.
World consumption of commercial energy sources

Source: OPEC, Facts and figures (Vienna, 1986).

60

Figure 21.
Per capita oil consumption

DCs   1.7 Barrels/person/y
Population : 2,550 million
Consumption : 11.6 million b/d

CPEs   3.4 Barrels/person/y

Population : 1,429 million
Consumption : 13.4 million b/d

DCs Developing countries
CPEs Centrally-planned economies

OECD   15.2 Barrels/person/y

Population : 808 million
Consumption : 33.5 million b/d

Source: OPEC, Facts and Figures (Vienna, 1986)

by the year 2050. It should be noted, however, that these and other energy forecasts depend on a number of different assumptions and different aggregating procedures that make them roughly indicative and subject to a wide range of error and changes.

170.   The 1970s brought about a general realization that fossil fuel resources, especially oil and natural gas, are finite and that countries should explore the possibilities of using other sources as well, establishing thereby an appropriate energy mix to meet their demands for sustainable development. Several scenarios have been proposed: expanded utilization of coal resources which are more abundant than those of oil and natural gas, development of non-conventional fossil fuels like oil shales and tar sands, further development of nuclear power, development of different renewable sources of energy, etc. (122, 123). However, the development of an appropriate energy mix depends on a number of factors: economic, environmental and geo-political that differ from one country to another.

171.   The 1970s also brought into focus a growing concern about the environmental impacts of energy production, transportation and use. Studies by UNEP (37, 124) and others have shown that of the many environmental impacts asssociated with any energy technology, some are significant and might affect different communities in different ways; others are not localized and might cross international boundaries affecting large regions; and others might have long-term effects. A comparative assessment of the environmental impacts of different sources of energy could not be made because of the inadequacy in our knowledge of many of these impacts for some sources of energy. A distinction should be made between the assessment of the nature, scale and geographic distribution of the impact, and the evaluation which is concerned with its value or importance.

172.   The recent drop in oil prices has raised fears that countries might embark on excessive consumption of oil, which would augment environmental problems associated with oil utilization. However, it should be noted that the developed countries (the major consumers) have already adjusted their energy-economy intensity over the past decade, and it is highly unlikely that they would reverse this trend. As for the developing countries, their high debt and serious economic status would preclude any substantial increase in oil consumption. The most immediate effect of drop in oil prices has been on the pace of development of renewable sources of energy, with several national programmes being affected. By the end of 1986, however, oil prices had started to rise again.

173.   An important development of the past decade has been the acceleration of ways and means to increase the efficiency of energy utilization in the developed countries. Research and development have increased the efficiency of many household technologies (126). In 1985, a United States study found that in the past decade the efficiency of new refrigerators increased 52 per cent and that of room air-conditioners 76 per cent. New Japanese and European fluorescent lights use one third as much power as systems now in use. It has been pointed out (126) that for seven countries (Denmark, France, Federal Republic of Germany, Sweden, Norway, United States and Canada), domestic oil use decreased by 40 per cent between 1972 and 1983, amounting to total savings of about 59 million t.o.e. per year. Substantial savings of energy have also been accomplished in the transport sector (paragraphs 118-125 above). In industry considerable progress has been made over the past decade. Japan provides a model of industrial energy efficiency: the energy intensities of chemical and steel production have dropped by 38 and 16 per cent, respectively, since 1973, and energy use per unit of output has fallen in every major sector since 1975 (75). The French industrial sector also ranks among the most energy-efficient, and, like Japan, made substantial improvements after 1973. Energy intensity in textiles, building materials, rubber and plastics, and mechanical construction fell by more than 30 per cent, an annual rate of improvement of more than 3.5 per cent. In the United States, the energy intensity of the production of paper, aluminium, steel and cement fell by 17 per cent between 1972 and 1982 (75).

174.   Energy efficiency has been far and away the largest contributor to the improved world oil situation during the past decade. Indeed, statistics show that greater efficiency accounts for over half the 36 per cent decline in the energy/GNP ratio of industrial countries since 1973. Between 1973 and 1984, United States energy efficiency rose 23 per cent. As can be seen from figure 22, Western Europe realized a 16 per cent decline in its energy intensity between 1973 and 1984, while Japan led the world with a remarkable 29 per cent decline in its energy/GNP ratio (125). Yet there is still enormous potential for further improvements in the energy efficiency of the world's economies.

Nuclear energy

175.   Electricity was first generated from nuclear reactors in 1954. The growth in capacity was slow until the early 1960s, but the number of new reactors ordered per year then rose dramatically to a peak in 1973 (about 75 reactors with capacities greater than 150 MW were ordered in that year), after which it fell equally dramatically for economic, environmental and social reasons (37). By March 1979, 186 nuclear reactors with a total capacity of 112 GW were in operation in 20 countries. The accident at Three Mile Island that occurred on 28 March 1979 has had its effect in slowing down nuclear programmes in several countries (especially in the United States). As a matter of fact the accident has augmented public concern about safety and the environmental impacts of nuclear power. The estimates that were originally made for nuclear power growth by the turn of the century had to be scaled down (127), and it now seems rather unlikely that the estimate made by the International Atomic Energy Agency (IAEA) in 1979 (1100-1700 GW by the year 2000) will be reached.

176.   At the end of 1985 there were 374 nuclear power plants, with a total capacity of about 250 GW, in operation in the world (see figure 23). In energy terms, nuclear power plants generated about 1400 terawatt-hours of electricity during 1985, and accounted for about 15 per cent of the world's electricity generation during 1985. The nuclear share in electricity generation varies greatly from country to country, and also from region to region in some countries (for example, in the United States). If present growth in nuclear power remains unaffected by the recent accident at Chernobyl*, the world-wide nuclear generating capacity may reach 370 GW by 1990.

177.   However, it should be noted that many of the issues that have aroused public opposition to nuclear power have still not been satisfactorily solved (124, 127). These issues cover the whole nuclear fuel cycle from mining and milling of the uranium ore to reactor operation and the disposal of radioactive wastes and range from socio-economic aspects to safety and environmental questions. The issues of safe disposal of high-level radioactive wastes and of liability and compensation in cases of accidents with transboundary impacts still remain without adequate solutions. Most of these issues can only be solved through international co-operation that emphasizes joint extensive research and information exchange.

* A detailed account of the accident that occurred in 1986 at Chernobyl, USSR, is contained in document UNEP/GC.14/10.

63

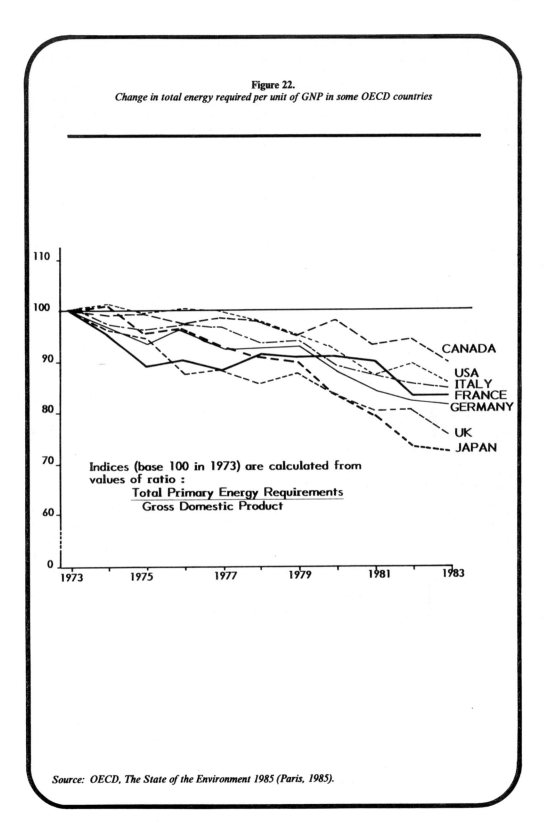

Figure 22.
Change in total energy required per unit of GNP in some OECD countries

CANADA
USA
ITALY
FRANCE
GERMANY
UK
JAPAN

Indices (base 100 in 1973) are calculated from values of ratio :
Total Primary Energy Requirements
Gross Domestic Product

Source: OECD, The State of the Environment 1985 (Paris, 1985).

64

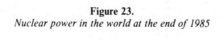

Figure 23.
Nuclear power in the world at the end of 1985

DCs — Developing countries
CPEs – Centrally-planned economies
INDUSTRIALIZED COUNTRIES

No. of Units in Operation

Megawatts

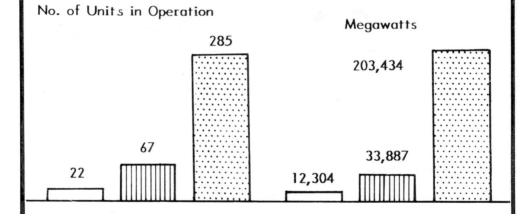

Source: Data supplied by the International Atomic Energy Agency.

ENVIRONMENTAL PROTECTION MEASURES

Public perception and attitude

National responses

International responses

ENVIRONMENTAL PROTECTION MEASURES

PUBLIC PERCEPTION AND ATTITUDE

178. The public's attitude towards the environment changed considerably after the Stockholm Conference. While remaining concerned about pollution, people became more aware of the scarcity of some natural resources, the necessity for conservation and the relationship between environment and development.

179. Public attitudes can affect the quality of the environment in at least two important ways. First, individuals can mobilize support for particular issues and exert political pressure that causes changes in public environmental policies. Secondly, public attitudes can affect the way individual members of society act in relation to the environment. The first is best illustrated by the flurry of pollution legislation and regulations that have been formulated and implemented in many countries over the past decade. The second has been important, for example, in promoting energy conservation in several countries and in the protection of wildlife and some other resources in others.

180. Public opinion surveys co-ordinated by OECD and carried out between 1981 and 1984, showed a significant common pattern in the United States, Japan and Europe: for example, despite the economic problems experienced by several OECD countries in that period, only about 27 per cent of the public was willing to sacrifice some degree of environmental improvement for economic growth when offered the choice (1). Expressed concern was greater for national and global environmental problems than for local ones. The surveys indicated that 45 per cent of the public have been concerned about damage from oil spills, 45 per cent about nuclear waste disposal, 43 per cent about industrial waste disposal, 38 per cent about transfrontier pollution, 35 per cent about water pollution, and 35 per cent about air pollution (1). These surveys pioneered the measurement of opinion about several global environmental problems, and the findings suggest that concern is quite high: for example, 36 per cent of the public expressed concern about extinction of some plants or animal species in the world, 36 per cent also expressed concern about the depletion of the world forest resources, while 30 per cent of the public have been concerned about possible climate changes brought about by increase in carbon dioxide and other greenhouse gases (1).

181. The OECD surveys also indicated that public opinion supporting environmental improvements has remained remarkably strong over time. Where public opinion polls have asked the same questions about environmental issues over a period of years, there has been little or no softening of support for stronger programmes in spite of either observable improvements in environmental quality or adverse economic circumstances. In the United States, for example, the support for stronger programmes has actually increased since 1980. In addition, polls in the United States, Japan and Finland show that large numbers of people believe things have worsened rather than improved over the past 10 years. In a survey conducted in the United States in 1982, 41 per cent of respondents said the quality of the environment had "grown worse" over the last 10 years compared with 29 per cent who believed it had "improved" and 28 per cent who felt it had "stayed the same".

182. On the other hand, public perception and attitude towards the environment in the developing countries vary widely from region to region and from country to country. There is, however, a common feature: concern is focused more on local and national problems

than on international issues. People are more concerned about water pollution, air pollution, municipal solid wastes, noise and to some extent about industrial wastes.

183. In general, awareness of human impact on the natural environment has grown rapidly since 1980. It has been manifest in countless conferences, meetings, publications, and debates. The news media and non-governmental organizations have been instrumental in promoting this increasing awareness. Many countries have now initiated television and other mass communications programmes to inform people about specific environmental issues and about their environmental responsibilities. In some countries, these efforts are sponsored substantially by the Government, while in others, non-governmental organizations have taken the lead

NATIONAL RESPONSES

184. The task of designing and implementing environmental protection programmes rests with national Government. At present, nearly all countries have environmental machineries of some kind. Some countries have established ministries for environment and/or natural resources; others have established environmental protection agencies and/or departments either as independent bodies or affiliated to particular ministries. The responsibilities of these environmental bodies vary from one country to another. In general, the function is to design programmes to protect the national environment through the enactment of legislation, the establishment of standards for levels of various emissions, the creation of monitoring programmes to identify where problems are most serious and to measure the success of the control programmes in dealing with them, and so forth. In some countries, periodical reports have been published since the early 1970s describing trends in air and water quality. Such environmental quality reports have been further developed by time to include other aspects of the environment and amount, at present, to national state-of-the-environment reports. Over the past five years, an increasing number of countries produced such reports, but few provide time-series data that can be used to establish trends in environmental quality. In addition, the information they contain is difficult to compare. In 1985, UNEP published guidelines for the preparation of national state-of-the-environment reports, in order to facilitate inter-country and inter-regional comparisons.

185. Although several countries formulated laws to improve the quality of their environment many decades ago, most of these have been amended, or clarified, in recent years. In some cases, changes were required because problems were found to be more serious than had originally been thought. In other cases, the adjustments were to make the environmental protection programmes more effective. However, it has not been easy to implement environmental laws. Sometimes, the environmental machinery in a country does not have sufficient information to know the extent to which polluters do or do not comply with the rules. Some countries have been unable to keep pace with their time tables for the implementation of environmental laws, particularly the developing countries, where environmental laws are hardly given effect.

186. Recently, some adjustments have been made to environmental laws and programmes in some countries. One approach was to adopt market-type economic incentives as part of the environmental control programmes. Such schemes may improve both the effectiveness and the efficiency of the existing laws. Under such a law, industrial companies in the Federal Republic of Germany had to begin paying taxes on their waste-water discharges in 1981 (1). Several countries have implemented noise taxes for aircraft or disposal charges for waste oil. The United States has allowed emission limitations to be traded among different sources in order to allow the most abatement to take place at the sources where it is least expensive, and

has also attempted to set non-compliance penalties to offset any cost savings that enterprises may make as a result of being in infraction.

187.   Several countries have been attempting to integrate their environmental protection programmes more closely with other programmes, for example, development programmes, natural resources management, and conservation programmes. Harvesting timber, for instance, can cause soil erosion and water pollution, eliminate scarce wild life habitat, and diminish the quality of recreation. Recognizing these conflicts, several countries are increasingly managing their natural resources in the light of a "multiple-use" concept that takes account of these different environmental values. In some countries, such as France, Hungary and Bulgaria, environmental programmes are included in economic plans. Others, such as the Federal Republic of Germany, the Netherlands, Canada, the United States, and the Nordic countries, include environmental analyses, to varying degrees, in the development assistance they provide to developing countries.

188.   Another important development in recent years is the increase of public participation in the decision-making process, especially in developed countries, through what has been known as environmental impact assessment processes. Although the details of these processes differ substantially from one country to another, they usually require that the environmental implications of a proposed action be analysed thoroughly, and that they are described in an impact statement made available to the public. They also include opportunities for the public to react to such proposals, and require that the agency responsible takes these reactions into account. Most of the bodies of legislation in OECD countries include provisions for undertaking such environmental impact assessments. On the other hand, environmental impacts assessments, including public participation, are hardly implemented in developing countries.

189.   One important conclusion that emerged from the UNEP report *The World Environment, 1972-1982* was that the environmental data base is of very variable quality and that there are startling gaps and a special lack of reliable quantitative information about the environment in the developing world. In addition, there has been a marked lack of time-series data and, therefore, the establishment of trends in environmental quality has been very difficult. OECD has recently pointed out that one of the most serious problems facing OECD countries as they attempt to implement their environmental programmes is the lack of information on current and past environmental conditions, and incomplete understanding of why some of the more serious environmental problems are occurring and what can be done to solve them. OECD further pointed out that there is a substantial need for more research and monitoring to allow more efficient responses, in order to keep better track of the progress being made and to allow better anticipation of emerging problems.

190.   Recognizing this need, several OECD countries have enacted special environmental research and monitoring statutes and established environmental research centres. Most countries also have large government-supported environmental research programmes. It has been estimated that in 1981, the OECD countries spent about 700 million on environmental research. Expenditures on environmental research vary in different countries and are generally between 0.3 and 3.0 per cent of total expenditure on research and development (1). Although some environmental research is being carried out in scattered research centres and universities in developing countries, no data are available for expenditures on it, since these are commonly included under other areas or in the overall expenditure on research and development.

191.   Supporting environmental research is not the only, or largest, purpose of government environmental expenditures. Other major purposes include municipal waste water treatment, residential solid waste collection and disposal, abatement of pollution from government-

owned facilities, the costs of management of natural resources, and so forth. A few countries have collected data on all of these expenditures: for example, in Hungary, investment in environmental protection increased from 2.5 per cent of total investment in the economic sector in 1980 to 3.4 per cent in 1984 (5), with about 45 per cent of investments going into water management, 31 per cent into industry, 15 per cent into agriculture, and the remainder into other sectors.

INTERNATIONAL RESPONSES

192.   The world economy in 1985 was characterized by modest expansion of production and disappointingly slow growth in international trade after the significant but uneven increases observed in 1984. The growth of world output fell back by nearly one third, from the rate of 4.6 per cent reached in 1984. The growth of world trade was only about one third of the near 9 per cent observed in 1984. Expected rates of growth of world output for 1986 and 1987 are of the order of 3.5 per cent. The rate of growth of world trade is expected to be somewhat above 4 per cent on average in 1986 and 1987 (128).

193.   Although the economic performance of the developed marked economies in 1985 was well below expectations, for most countries in the group the recovery continued. For several countries, it entered its fourth year in early 1986. A remarkable feature of this recovery, aside from its durability, is that significant expansion of output has taken place simultaneously with a sharp reduction in the rate of inflation in nearly all countries in the group. In the period 1983-1985, for the group as a whole, real output grew by 10.5 per cent while the inflation rate fell by 3 percentage points (128).

194.   On the other hand, events in 1985 demonstrated once again the vulnerability of many developing countries to external events, which has increased partly as a result of inadequate external financing. The slow-down in the growth of the developed countries was costly and untimely for all those developing countries whose fortunes arc closely tied to international trade. After some progress in 1984, these countries suffered a major set-back in 1985. The rate of increase in their export volume fell significantly, their terms of trade worsened and for many of them interest rates in real terms rose sharply. For the developing countries as a whole, the growth rate of GDP remained below 2.5 per cent for the fifth year in a row. Nearly 60 per cent of the developing countries, in Africa and Latin America, had either stagnant or falling real per capita GDP in 1985 (128).

195.   While the state of the world environment is not directly dependent on short-term economic fluctuations, it cannot be considered to be isolated from them. Owing to the financial strains to which the developed countries have been exposed during the years of recession, there has evidently been less readiness and capacity on their part to deal with the problems of environmental improvement in the developing countries or indeed in the developed countries themselves.

196.   The world community is confronted by a closed cycle: economic problems cause environmental despoliation which, in turn, makes economic and structural reform more difficult to achieve. Breaking the cycle requires a new earnestness from nations in their approach to environmental co-operation. Two major causes of environmental destruction should be tackled now. First, the arms race, with its insatiable demands on global financial, material and intellectual resources, must be slowed down. The second requirement that the appalling debt burden of many developing countries should be alleviated.

197.   Global military expenditure has increased more than 30-fold since 1900. In 1985, the world's military expenditure was estimated to be about $US663 billion (at 1980 prices and exchange rates, or about $850-870 billion in current 1985 dollars)—about $1.7 million every

minute in current dollars (129). The upward trend has accelerated in recent years. During the 1970s, military expenditure increased in real terms at an average annual rate of 2.5 per cent. Since 1980, however, the average real rise was 3.5 per cent a year (130). Besides its colossal financial implications, military activity exerts increasing pressures on human and natural resources.

198.   The introduction of nuclear weapons has added entirely new dimensions to warfare. Quantitatively, it has brought an enormous increase in explosive power over that of conventional weapons. It has been estimated that there are now between 37,000 and 50,000 nuclear warheads in the world, with a total explosive power of between 11,000 and 20,000 megatons (equivalent to between 846,000 and 1,540,000 Hiroshima bombs). Recent studies (131-142), in spite of several uncertainties, estimate that about 750 million people would be killed outright by the blast alone, while about 1.1 billion would be killed by the combined effects of the blast, fire and radiation and the same number again would suffer injuries requiring medical attention. In the aftermath of the nuclear war, darkened skies would cover large areas of the Earth for several months, temperatures might drop to below freezing for varying periods of time, the so-called "nuclear winter", and climatic disturbances might persist for years. All this would severely affect major ecosystems in the world, leading to wide-scale disruption in bioproductivity and spreading famines over vast areas in both combatant and non-combatant nations.

199.   There are some obvious contradictions in the attitude of the world community to the whole question of military activity. On one hand, the numerous conventions, treaties, and agreements provide clear evidence of a widespread desire to prevent the more devastating forms of warfare. On the other, the evidence of mounting military expenditure around the world implies a lack of conviction in the practicability of disarmament, or even of holding forces and arsenals at constant size. And there are further contradictions between the demands for agricultural, social and economic development so vital to the future of the world, in particular to the developing countries, and the increasing allocation of limited resources for military purposes.

200.   The expectations for multinational co-operation raised at different forums over the last ten years have not yet been fulfilled. The global negotiations, whose immediate launching has been called for, have not materialized. The results of the Sixth United Nations Conference on Trade and Development have been disappointing for many, particularly the developing countries, and a similar disappointment has been felt over the failure to translate into concrete action the prescriptions for global economic recovery made out at various summit meetings.

201.   In the field of the environment, the preparedness of Governments to translate good intentions into action has been more positive *. The World Conservation Strategy, the World Charter for Nature, the Vienna Convention for the Protection of the Ozone Layer, and the different conventions for the protection of the marine environment and coastal areas in different regions are illustrations of international support for environmental protection. However, there is still an urgent need for the world community to translate these good intentions into practical actions. This is particularly true for the implementation of world plans of action such as those relating to desertification control, soils policy, conservation strategies, the protection of regional marine environments, and so forth.

---

*   *See the UNEP "Register of international treaties and other agreements in the field of the environment".*

REFERENCES

REFERENCES

1. OECD, *The State of the Environment 1985* (Paris, OECD Publications, 1985).

2. *Oxides of Nitrogen,* Environmental Health Criteria, No. 4 (Geneva, WHO, 1977);*Sulphur Oxides and Suspended Particulate Matter,* Environmental Health Criteria, No. 8 (Geneva, WHO, 1979);*Carbon Monoxide,* Environmental Health Criteria, No. 13 (Geneva, WHO, 1979).

3. B.G. Bennett and others, "Urban air pollution worldwide", *Environmental Science and Technology,* vol. 19 (1985), p.298.

4. G. Pavlov, *The Protection and Improvement of the Environment in the People's Republic of Bulgaria* (Moscow, CMEA Committee for Scientific and Technological Co-operation, 1982).

5. *State and Protection of the Environment* (Budapest, Kozponti Statisztikai Hivatal, 1986).

6. D.M. Whelpdale, "Acid deposition: distribution and impact", *Water Quality Bulletin,* vol.8, No. 2 (April 1983), p.72.

7. H. W. Georgii, *Review of the Chemical Composition of Precipitation as Measured by the WMO BAPMoN* (Geneva, WMO, 1982).

8. United States Environmental Protection Agency, *The Acidic Deposition Phenomenon and its Effects* (Washington, D.C., 1984).

9. J. Harte, "An investigation of acid precipitation in Qinghai Province, China", *Atmospheric Environment,* vol. 17, No. 2 (1983), p.403.

10. J. McCormick, *Acid Earth* (London, Earthscan, IIED, 1985).

11. D. Zhao and B. Sun, "Air pollution and acid rain in China", *Ambio,* vol.15, No. 2 (1986).

12. G.L. Brady and J.C. Selle, "Acid rain: the international response", *International Journal of Environmental Studies,* vol.24 (1985), p.217.

13. Environment Canada, *State of the Environment Report for Canada* (Ottawa, 1986).

14. P. Middleton and S.L. Rhodes, "Acid rain and drinking water degradation", *Environmental Monitoring and Assessment,* vol.4 (1984), p.44.

15. M.E. McDonald, "Acid deposition and drinking water", *Environmental Science and Technology,* vol.19 (1985), p.772.

16. A. Grimvall and others, "Quality trends of public water supplies in Sweden", *Water Quality Bulletin,* vol.11, No.6 (1986).

17. United Nations, Economic Commission for Europe, *Airborne Sulphur Pollution,* Air Pollution Studies No.1 (Geneva, 1984).

18. L.W. Blank, "A new type of forest decline in Germany", *Nature,* vol.314 (March-April 1985), p.311.

19. W.O. Binns, "Effects of acidic deposition on forests and soils", *The Environmentalist,* vol.5, No.4 (Winter 1985), p.279.

20. B. Nihlgard, "The ammonium hypothesis an additional explanation for the forest dieback in Europe", *Ambio, vol.14, No.1 (1985), p.2.*

21. *WHO Working Group, "Health impact of acidic deposition", The Science of the Total Environment,* vol.52, No.3 (July 1986).

22. A.A. Moghissi, "Potential public health impacts of acidic deposition", *Water Quality Bulletin,* vol.11, No.3 (1986).

23. *Changing Climate,* report of the Carbon Dioxide Assessment Committee, National Research Council (Washington, D.C., National Academy Press, 1983).

24. *Report of the International Conference on the Assessment of the Role of Carbon Dioxide and of Other Greenhouse Gases in Climate Variations and Associated Impacts,* WMO report No.661 (1986).

25. B. Bolin and others, eds., *The Greenhouse Effect, Climatic Change and Ecosystems (Scope: 29)* (Chichester, John Wiley and Sons, 1986).

26. A. Neftel and others, "Evidence from polar ice cores for the increase in atmospheric carbon dioxide in the past two centuries", *Nature,* vol.315 (May-June 1985), p.45.

27. WMO/NASA, *Atmospheric Ozone 1985,* Global Ozone Research and Monitoring Project Report No. 16 (Geneva, WMO, 1985).

28. V. Ramanathan and others, "Trace gas trends and their potential role in climate change", *Journal of Geophysical Research,* vol. 90 (1985).

29. R.A. Rasmussen and M.A. Khalil, "The behaviour of trace gases in the troposphere", *The Science of the Total Environment,* vol.48, No.3 (February 1986).

30. D.H. Ehhalt, "Methane in the global atmosphere", *Environment,* vol.27, No.10 (December 1985).

31. "Report of the eighth session of the Co-ordinating Committee on the Ozone Layer" (UNEP/CCOL/VIII).

32. J. Lemons, "Carbon dioxide and the environment: a problem of uncertainty", *Journal of Environmental Science* (March-April 1985).

33. B.A. Kimball, "Carbon dioxide and agricultural yield; an assemblage and analysis of 430 prior observations", *Agronomy Journal,* vol.75 (1983), p.779.

34. B.A. Kimball and S.B. Idso, "Increasing atmospheric carbon dioxide: effects on crop yield, water use and climate", *Agricultural Water Management,* vol.7 (1983), p.55.

35. "Executive summary prepared by the International Meteorological Institute in Stockholm", *Report of the International Conference on the Assessment of the Role of Carbon Dioxide and of other Greenhouse Gases in Climate Variations and Associated Impacts,* WMO report No.661 (1986).

36. M.J. Prather and others, "Reductions in ozone at high concentrations of stratospheric halogens", *Nature,* vol.312 (November-December 1984), p.227.

37. UNEP, *The World Environment 1972-1982* (Dublin, Tycooly International, 1982).

38. WRI/IIED, *World Resources 1986* (New York, Basic Books, 1986).

39. G. Thomas, *Organization of Environmental Protection in the German Democratic Republic* (Moscow, CMEA Committee for Scientific and Technical Co-operation, 1982).

40. National Research Council, *Ground Water Quality Protection* (Washington D.C., National Academy Press, 1986).

41. P.W. Holden, *Pesticides and Ground Water Quality* (Washington, D.C., National Academy Press, 1986).

42. D.E. Burmaster, "Ground water: saving the unseen resource", *Environment,* vol.28 (1986), p.25.

43. J.H. Foegen, "Contaminated water", *The Futurist* (March-April 1986), p.22.

44. F.L.O. Deck, "Community water supply and sanitation in developing countries, 1970-1990", *World Health Statistics Quarterly,* vol.39 (1986), No.1, p.2.

45. UNICEF/WHO Joint Committee on Health Policy, twenty fifth session, document JC25/UNICEF-WHO/ 85 6 (b) (1985).

46. N.W. Schmidtke, "Water pollution control technology in Canada", *Water Quality Bulletin,* vol.7, No.3 (July 1982).

47. P. Balmer, "Water pollution control in Sweden", *Water Quality Bulletin,* vol.7, No.3 (July 1982).

48. T. Kubo, "Water pollution control technology in Japan", *Water Quality Bulletin,* vol.8, No.4 (October 1983).

49. R.L. Bunch, "Water pollution control technology in the USA", *Water Quality Bulletin,* vol.7, No.3 (July 1982).

50. FAO, "The state of food and agriculture 1986", document CL 9O/2 (Rome, 1986).

51. FAO, *Land, Food and People* (Rome, 1984).

52. UNEP/FAO, *Guidelines for the Control of Soil Degradation* (Rome, FAO, 1983).

53. M.K. Tolba, "A harvest of dust?", *Environmental Conservation* vol.11, No.1, (Spring 1984).

54. E. El-Hinnawi, *Environmental Refugees* (Nairobi, UNEP, 1985).

55. D. Pimentel and others, "Land degradation: effects on food and energy resources", *Science*, vol.194, No.4261 (8 October 1976).

56. E. El-Hinnawi and A.K. Biswas, *Renewable Sources of Energy and the Environment* (Dublin, Tycooly International, 1981).

57. G.T. Goodman, "Energy and development: where do we go from here?", *Ambio*, vol.24, No.4-5 (1985), p.186.

58. K. Openshaw, "Woodfuel a time for re-assessment", *Natural Resources Forum*, vol.3 (1978), p.35.

59. K. Openshaw, "Energy requirements for household cooking in Africa with existing and improved cooking stoves", *Proceedings of BioEnergy '80 Congress* (Washington D.C., BioEnergy Council, 1980).

60. FAO, *Yearbook of Forest Products 1972-1983* (Rome, 1985).

61. J. Melillo and others, "Comparison of two recent estimates of disturbances in tropical forests", *Environmental Conservation*, vol.12 (1985), p.37.

62. FAO, *Fuelwood Supplies in Developing Countries* (Rome, 1983).

63. UNEP, *Asia-Pacific Report: The Resources of Development* (Nairobi, 1981).

64. E.O. Wilson, "The biological diversity crisis", *Issues in Science and Technology*, vol.II, No.1 (Fall 1985) p.20.

65. S. Zhigzh, *Protection of the Environment and Rational Use of Natural Resources in the Mongolian People's Republic* (Moscow, CMEA Committee for Scientific and Technical Co-operation, 1982).

66. *A Concise Report on the World Population Situation in 1983: Conditions, Trends, Prospects and Policies*, Population Studies, No.85 (ST/ESA/SER.A/85).

67. World Bank, *World Development Report 1984* (Washington D.C., 1984).

68. UNICEF, *The State of the World's Children* (Geneva, 1986).

69. Julian L. Simon, *The Ultimate Resource* (Princeton, Princeton University Press, 1981).

70. Julian L. Simon and H. Khan, *The Resourceful Earth* (Oxford, Blackwell, 1984).

71. United Nations Centre for Human Settlements (Habitat), *Survey of Slum and Squatter Settlements* (Dublin, Tycooly International, 1982).

72. L.R. Brown, "Reconsidering the automobile's future", *State of the World 1984*, L.R. Brown and others, eds. (New York, W.W. Norton and Co., 1984).

73. UNCTAD, *Review of Maritime Transport 1984* (Geneva, 1985).

74. D. Bayliss, *Automobile Traffic in Developing Countries: Environmental and Health Issues*, WHO report No. EFP/EC/WP/83.4 (Geneva, 1983).

75. W.V. Chandler, "Increasing energy efficiency", *State of the World 1985*, L.R. Brown and others, eds. (New York, W.W. Norton and Co., 1985).

76. International Energy Agency, *Fuel Efficiency of Passenger Cars* (Paris, International Energy Agency, OECD, 1984).

77. C.L. Ndiokwere, "A study of heavy metal pollution from motor vehicle emissions and its effect on roadside soil, vegetation and crops in Nigeria", *Environmental Pollution (Series B)*, vol.7 (1984), No.1.

78. A. Falahi-Ardakani, "Contamination of environment with heavy metal emitted from automobiles", *Ecotoxicology and Environmental Quality*, vol.8 (1984), p.152.

79. R. Pasquini and S. Monarca, "Detection of mutagenic/carcinogenic compounds in unused and used motor oils", *The Science of the Total Environment* vol.32, No.1 (December 1983).

80. R.G. Cuddihy and others, "Health risks from light-duty vehicles", *Environmental Science and Technology,* vol.18 (1984), p.14A.

81. A. Haulot, "The environment and the social value of tourism", *The International Journal of Environmental Studies,* vol.25, No.4 (1985), p.219.

82. R.V. Salm, "Integrating marine conservation and tourism", *The International Journal of Environmental Studies,* vol.25, No.4 (1985).

83. D.G. Pearce and R.M. Kirk, "Carrying capacities for coastal tourism", *Industry and Environment,* vol.9, No.1 (January/February/March 1986), p.3.

84. I. Jackson, "Carrying capacity for tourism in small tropical Caribbean islands", *Industry and Environment,* vol.9, No.1 (January/February/March 1986), p.7.

85. R.V. Salm, "Coral reefs and tourist carrying capacity: the Indian Ocean experience", *Industry and Environment,* vol.9, No.1 (January/February/March 1986), p.11.

86. D. Western, "Tourist capacity in East African parks", *Industry and Environment,* vol.9, No.1 (January/February/March 1986), p.14.

87. J.J. Lindsay, "Carrying capacity for tourist development in national parks of the United States", *Industry and Environment,* vol.9, No.1 (January/February/March 1986), p.17.

88. T.V. Singh and J. Kaur, "The paradox of mountain tourism: case references from the Himalaya", *Industry and Environment,* vol.9, No.1 (January/February/March 1986), p.21.

89. FAO, *The State of Food and Agriculture 1984* (Rome, 1985).

90. World Bank, *The World Development Report 1982* (Washington D.C., 1982).

91. World Bank, *The World Development Report 1986* (Washington D.C., 1986).

92. D. Gale Johnson, "World food and agriculture", *The Resourceful Earth,* J.L. Simon and H. Khan, eds. (Oxford, Blackwell, 1984).

93. R. Revelle, "The world supply of agricultural land", *The Resourceful Earth,* J.L. Simon and H. Khan, eds. (Oxford, Blackwell, 1984).

94. N.C. Brady, "Chemistry and the world food supply", Science, vol.218, No.4575 (26 November 1982).

95. A.K. Biswas and others, eds., *Long-Distance Water Transfer,* Water Resources Series, vol.3, (Dublin, Tycooly International, 1983).

96. FAO, *Fertilizer Yearbook,* vol.34 (Rome, 1984).

97. O.P. Engelstad, "Crop nutrition technology", *Future Agricultural Technology and Resource Conservation,* B.C. English and others, eds. (Ames, Iowa, Iowa State University Press, 1984).

98. Economic Commission for Europe, *Market Trends for Chemical Products, 1975-1980, and Prospects for 1990* (ECE/CHEM/4O, vol.1).

99. D. Pimentel and L. Levitan, "Pesticides: amounts applied and amounts reaching pests", *BioScience,* vol.36 (1986), p.86.

100. D. Bull, *Pesticides and the Third World: A Growing Problem* (London, Oxfam, 1982).

101. G.P. Georghiou and R.B. Mellon, "Pesticide resistance in time and space", *Pest Resistance to Pesticides,* G.P.Georghiou and R.B. Mellon, eds. (New York, Plenum Press, 1983).

102. M.J. Dover and B.A. Croft, "Pesticide resistance and public policy", *BioScience,* vol.36 (l986), p.78.

103. R. Repetto, *Paying the Price: Pesticide Subsidies in Developing Countries,* research report No. 2 (Washington D.C., World Resources Institute, 1985).

104. National Research Council, *Genetic Engineering of Plants* (Washington D.C., National Academy Press, 1984).

105. G.B. Collins and J.G. Petolino, *Applications of Genetic Engineering to Crop Improvement* (Dordrecht, Martinus Nijhoff/W. Junk, 1984).

106. A. Sasson, *Biotechnologies: challenges and promises,* Sextant No. 2 (Paris, UNESCO, 1984).

107. E. Bjurstrom, "Biotechnology", *Chemical Engineering* (18 February 1985).

108. M. Hansen and others, "Plant breeding and biotechnology", *BioScience,* vol. 36 (1986), p.29.

109. M.D. Dibner, "Biotechnology in Europe", *Science,* vol.232 (April-June 1986), p.1365.

110. W.J. Brill, "Safety concerns and genetic engineering in agriculture", *Science,* vol.227 (January-March 1985), p.381.

111. R.K. Colwell and others, "Genetic engineering in agriculture", *Science,* vol. 229 (July-September 1985), p.111.

112. W. Szybalski, "Comments on Brill's article", *Science,* vol.229 (July-September 1985), p.112.

113. OECD, *Recombinant DNA Safety Considerations* (Paris, 1986).

114. L.R. Brown, "Maintaining world fisheries", *State of the World 1985,* L.R. Brown and others, eds. (New York, W.W. Norton and Co., 1985).

115. R.A. Neal, "Aquaculture expansion and environmental considerations", *Mazingira,* vol.8, No.3 (July 1984), p.24.

116. UNIDO, *Industry and Development: Global Report 1986* (Vienna, 1986).

117. M. Dowling, "Defining and classifying hazardous wastes", *Environment,* vol.27 (1985), p.18.

118. T. Kean, "Dealing with toxic air pollutants: new initiatives", *Issues in Science and Technology,* vol.2, No.4 (Summer 1986), p.19.

119. WHO, *Management of Hazardous Wastes,* WHO Regional Publication No.14, European Series (Copenhagen, WHO Regional Office for Europe, 1983).

120. Council on Environmental Quality, *Environmental Quality 1984* (Washington D.C., 1984).

121. "The state of the environment: selected topics 1983" (UNEP/GC.11/4).

122. E. El-Hinnawi, "The promise of renewable sources of energy", *Renewable Sources of Energy and the Environment,* E. El-Hinnawi and A.K. Biswas, eds. (Dublin, Tycooly International, 1981).

123. E. El-Hinnawi and others, *New and Renewable Sources of Energy* (Dublin, Tycooly International, 1983).

124. UNEP, *The Environmental Impacts of Production and Use of Energy* (Dublin, Tycooly International, 1981).

125. C. Flavin, "Moving beyond oil", *State of the World 1986,* L.R. Brown and others, eds. (New York, W.W. Norton and Co., 1986).

126. L. Schipper and A.N. Ketoff, "The international decline in household oil use", *Science,* vol.230 (October-December 1985), p.1118.

127. E. El-Hinnawi, *Nuclear Energy and the Environment* (Oxford, Pergamon Press, 1980).

128. *World Economic Survey 1986,* (United Nations publication, Sales No. E.86. II C.1).

129. Stockholm International Peace Research Institute, *Yearbook 1986* (Stockholm, 1986).

130. Stockholm International Peace Research Institute, *Yearbook 1985* (Stockholm, 1985).

131. P.R. Ehrlich and others, "Long-term biological consequences of nuclear war", *Science, vol.222, (October-December 1983), p.1293.*

132. *R.P. Turco and others, "Nuclear winter: global consequences of multiple nuclear explosions", Science,* vol.222 (October-December 1983), p.1283.

133. R.P. Turco and others, "The climatic effects of nuclear war", *Scientific American,* vol.251, No.2 (August 1984), p.33.

134. A. Ehrlich, "Nuclear winter", *Bulletin of Atomic Scientists* (April 1984), p.35.

135. H.D. Grover, "The climatic and biological consequences of nuclear war", *Environment,* vol.26, No.4 (May 1984), p.7.

136. "Climatic effects of nuclear war" (United Nations General Assembly document A/40/449).

137. National Research Council, *The Effects on the Atmosphere of a Major Nuclear Exchange* (Washington D.C., National Academy Press, 1985).

138. Y.M. Svirezhev, *Ecological and Demographic Consequences of Nuclear War* (Moscow, USSR Academy of Sciences, 1985).

139. SCOPE, *Environmental Consequences of Nuclear War. Vol. II: Ecological and Agricultural Effects* (Chichester, John Wiley and Sons, 1986).

140. SCOPE, *Environmental Consequences of Nuclear War. vol.I: Physical and Atmospheric Effects* (Chichester, John Wiley and Sons, 1986).

141. L. Dotto, *Planet Earth in Jeopardy* (Chichester, John Wiley and Sons, 1986).

142. J. Peterson, "Scientific studies of the unthinkable—the physical and biological effects of nuclear war", *Ambio,* vol.15, No.1, (1986), p.60.